To Samina and Nick,

13.08.23

KAILASH:

Pilgrimages to the Tibetan Mystic Mountain

Heli Grauberg 2016 & 2019
Translator: Sireliis Vilu

I dedicate this book to Mount Kailash.

Author: Heli Grauberg
Translator: Sireliis Vilu (Estonian to English)
Editor: Erin N.
Cover photo: Shutterstock, Sundar Photo
Book design by Heli Grauberg

Copyright © Heli Grauberg, 2023. All rights reserved
No part of this book may be used or reproduced in any graphic, electronic, mechanical, or other form, except for brief quotations and with proper citation in articles and reviews, without the written permission of the author.

Contents

Introduction 1

PART I

MOUNT KAILASH & PILGRIMAGE

Organising my first pilgrimage.. 3

Mount Kailash 7

Kailash *inner kora,* or inner circle... 12

What is a pilgrimage?... 18

Monasteries around Mount Kailash.. 22

Inspiring books by Russian doctor and scientist Ernst Muldashev 25

The incredible story of Tracey Alysson 30

Prices 33

What to pack.. 36

Mountain sickness 39

Sherpas 42

INTERESTING FACTS ABOUT NEPAL

Nepal 43

The capital: Kathmandu 46

The Goddess Kumari 49

Earthquake in 2015 51

Mount Everest, or Jomolungma 52

Yeti 55

Hippies 57

Murder in the Royal household 58

Caste system 59

Marriage 60

Same-sex marriage 60

Temple of Pashupatinath 61

Writer and doctor Ernst Muldashev in the Nepali Embassy in 1999 65

INTERESTING FACTS ABOUT TIBET

Tibet 67

Dalai Lama Tenzin Gyatso 70

Panchen Lama 74

Buddhism in Tibet 75

Rules for entering Tibet 78

Etiquette and taboos 79

Tibetan kitchen 80

Yaks 82

The eagle, a holy bird 84

Tibetan mastiff 85

Rural marriage – polyandry (having several husbands) 86

Sky burial 87

PILGRIMAGE TO MOUNT KAILASH 2016

The trip begins in the capital of Nepal – Kathmandu. Visiting Boudhanath 92

First internal flight – Nepalgunj 97

Acclimatising at the home of a Nepalese family in Simikot 97

Helicopter flight to a Nepal-China border village, Hilsa 100

Acclimatising in Purang. Visiting the Gongphur cave monastery 103

The pilgrimage begins in Darchen 109

Days 1 and 2 of the pilgrimage 111

Day 3 of pilgrimage 116

Last, 4th day of the pilgrimage 120

"Lucky coin" from Lake Manasarovar and the nighttime nightmare 122

Glance on the Demonic Lake Rakshastal 127

Back to Hilsa and waiting several nights and days for a helicopter 128

In the middle of the runway at Simikot, waiting for a flight back 130

Miracle plane flight from Nepalgunj 131

Back to Kathmandu and a trip back home 131

Epilogue for Part I 132

PART II

PILGRIMAGE TO MOUNT KAILASH 2019

Decision to go on a new pilgrimage 137

Asking for blessings for my pilgrimage at the Shiva *havan* fire ceremony at Lilleoru 140

Arrival in Nepal 146

Excursion to the Manakamana temple 147

Visit to Boudhanath stupa and the house of the child goddess Kumari Ghar 155
My handmade silver jewellery in the expanses of Mount Kailash 159
The tour begins! Visiting Budhanilkantha temple and Pashupatinath 160
The ride to Tibet begins! Guru Purnima 163
Gurus 167
The chocolate egg problem at the Chinese border 172
Confusion with Chinese military officials 176
At Lake Manasarovar, waiting for the gods dance 179
One of the trip's highlights – through difficulties to blessings 183
Two adventures in one day – 1st day of *kora* and a hike to Charan Sparsh 189
2nd and 3rd day of *kora* – God Shiva, if you want, take me! 193
Sleep is back! 206
The trip comes to an end 210
Balancing the bus on the edge of a gorge back to Kathmandu 213
If ever again… 214
Visiting Swayambhunath 214
Really, back to Mount Kailash with a Nepali Baba?! 216
The ride back home 218
Acknowledgments 223
Synopsis 225
About the author 227

Prayer bells next to the Manakamana temple, Nepal. Heli Grauberg, 2019

Introduction

Mount Kailash in Tibet, Lake Manasarovar, and other sacred sites around it are symbols for followers of Hinduism, Buddhism, Jainism, and Bon. The whole book is written from a Hindu perspective, as I was surrounded only by Hindus on these pilgrimages, and yoga and Hinduism are closely intertwined.

I was inspired to write this book by a wish to share my experience gained in the centre of this faraway universe; I also thought about all those future pilgrims who would someday begin their journey to Mountain Kailash and could find some guidance in the information here.

NB! Many of the facts and stories in this book are from different sources: my own experiences and observations, tour guides and Sherpas of Nepal and Tibet, booklets picked up on the trip, the Internet (including the websites of Nepalese and Tibetan travel agencies) and books. I don't claim that all the years, heights, and other facts are completely accurate, because so often, the correct statistics are missing, and the information varies in different publications and sources.

PART I

MOUNT KAILASH & PILGRIMAGE

Organising my first pilgrimage

Fifteen years ago, I placed a picture of the sacred Tibetan Mount Kailash on the altar of my yoga room, hoping to attract a pilgrimage to this mystical land. Years passed, but I never felt it was the right time to go to the mountain. At the beginning of 2016, when I felt the right moment had arrived, I contacted Krishna, owner of a Nepali travel agency, who had helped me during my earlier travels in Nepal, and booked a pilgrimage planned for June—six months ahead.

Half a year is enough time to get into good physical shape. I had big plans for training, but in the end, I limited myself to light yoga. It also gave me time to save up some money, because the deposit for the Nepali travel agency for securing a place cost 300 USD, with the remainder to be paid there.

Before going on the trip, I left my partner a closed envelope with my bank card's PIN codes and my Facebook password, because I had heard and read lots of stories about accidents related to high-altitude sickness. If something were to go wrong, he could have closed my social media account, and paid off some of my bills.

A guru from India, Yogiraj Gurunath Siddhanath (see "Gurus" in Part II), was sharing his wisdom in London in June 2016. There was a meeting with Siddhanath Yoga Sangh (I have occasionally been involved with this yoga organisation) at which Gurunath gave me blessings for my first Mount Kailash pilgrimage ever. I felt them throughout my trip; it really worked.

Tibet has been under the rule of the People's Republic of China (PRC) since 1950-1951, and all travel plans are at the whim and direction of Chinese officials. My first pilgrimage was supposed to take me from Nepal to Tibet by highway, which would have provided plenty of time to acclimate and is much cheaper than a flight. But then I got a notification from the travel company that China doesn't permit highway travel and the Kailash Area can only be accessed via air: with several internal flights and a helicopter. Well, I guess I had to fly.

The next e-mail informed me that the Chinese officials wouldn't give permission for foreigners to access the area of Mount Kailash during the time when I had planned to be in Nepal.

So, the plane ticket to Nepal had to be changed so that I would arrive on one of the dates that were written on the freshly released entrance permission for the Kailash region.

Upon arriving in Nepal, I discovered that the group I was supposed to be in was already on its way to Kailash. Though one usually meets their pilgrimage group in the Nepali capital, Kathmandu, I met only with the travel agency's owner, Krishna, in the beginning, and because of the Chinese game rules, I was a lonely pilgrim for five or six days in Nepal. Luckily, the situation turned around. Because Krishna couldn't place me in any other group, he decided to give me a personal guide, so I could join some other agencies' pilgrimage groups later. My travel route was to be Kathmandu-Nepalgunj-Simikot-Hilsa-Purang-Darchen-Dirapuk-Zutulpuk-Darchen-Manasarovar.

On the way to the foot of Mount Kailash, Charan Sparsh, Tibet.
Umesh Giri, 2016

Animal skull with horns at Lake Manasarovar, Tibet.
Heli Grauberg, 2019

Mount Kailash

Mount Kailash in Western Tibet is one of the holiest mountains and one of the most sacred pilgrimage places on Earth. Known to some as the Centre of the Universe, it is a pyramid-shaped mountain rising 6638 meters (by some data 6666 m) into the sky, each facet facing a different cardinal point. It is covered in snow all year long. It's a uniting symbol for followers of Hinduism, Buddhism, Jainism and Bon.

A home for ancient wise men and gods, invisible to the human eye, whose knowledge, discoveries and work are gathered in this mountain. According to Hindu belief, Shiva, the god of yogis, both destructive and creative, lives on Mount Kailash, along with his wife Parvati. Each religion that worships Mount Kailash has its own beliefs about the place. The four great rivers of Asia – the Karnali, the Brahmaputra, the Indus and the Sutlej – all begin from that mountain.

Climbing Mount Kailash is strictly forbidden due to the religious significance of the mountain. There are many legends about people who have tried to conquer the mountain and lost their lives to it. There are also stories from the 19th century and the beginning of the 20th in which Russian mountaineers tried to climb Mount Kailash and disappeared in mysterious ways.

Another group that wanted to conquer the sacred mountain experienced an extremely rapid aging process, followed by a quick death. Traditional beliefs say that only a person free of all sins can conquer the mountain. Allegedly, the only person who has been to the top of the mountain was an 11th century Tibetan monk and yogi, Milarepa.

Traditionally, a 52-kilometre pilgrimage round, called a *kora* or *parikrama,* is made around the mountain clockwise over three days. The highest point during this journey is approximately 5630 meters above sea level. Only the Bon followers do the *kora* counterclockwise. Extremely dedicated pilgrims lie fully prostrate when doing *kora* and rise up only to lie down again at the point to which their hands had stretched. The repetition of this motion can last for weeks. Doing the circle around the mountain washes you of all sins and heals your karma. Twelve rounds will supposedly free you from your sins committed in this life and your previous one, and 108 rounds will give you a chance to get from reincarnation to *nirvana.* Those who walk around Mount Kailash will supposedly experience the wakening of their inner self and go through a spiritual cleansing. For some, walking around the mountain is a meditational form of exercise, and for others, it's just a big adventure. Some pilgrims limit themselves to looking at Mount Kailash from Lake Manasarovar. They take it as a *darshan*—a blessing and an experience of divine presence.

Making the trip to Kailash by foot and bowing to the sacred place is a matter of honour for every Tibetan – it's considered the purpose of life. Sometimes it takes over a year, because Tibet is big, and home can be far away. Sometimes, you get tired and go back to try again next year. Pilgrimage around Mount Kailash is made several times in a lifetime. Some brave Tibetan women take the trip during their last months of pregnancy so they can give birth to the baby as close as possible to the sacred mountain.

Brave Spanish alpineer Jesus Martinez Novas planned to broadcast a message of peace from the centre of the universe, the home of gods: the peak of Mount Kailash (2001). It sounds unbelievable, but China actually gave him permission. But after receiving a flood of criticism, the Spaniard tossed the plan aside.

A legendary Italian alpineer, Reinhold Messner, has placed in the *Guinness Book of World Records* several times, being the first man in the world to conquer all fourteen 8000-metre mountains and the only one to conquer Mount Everest alone. He also conquered the highest peak without an oxygen tank. In the 1980s, China offered him a chance to ascend to the peak of the holiest mountain – Kailash. Reinhold Messner said no. This is what he had to say about the Spaniard's plans to conquer the mountain: "If we conquer the mountain, we conquer something in the souls of the people. I suggest taking on something more difficult. Kailash is not that high and difficult."

The Chinese government had planned to build a highway around Mount Kailash in the spring of 2004 to boost tourism. This would certainly have destroyed the surrounding countryside and disrupted traditional rituals. The project received worldwide criticism and an avalanche of protest letters, and the Chinese government eventually abandoned the idea. It's possible that a UNESCO World Heritage nomination could help to prevent such plans in the future, and the Chinese government can apply for this nomination itself.

The 2011 Tibet edition of the world-famous *Lonely Planet* series of travel books, created by Maureen and Tony Wheeler, places Mount Kailash at the top of the list in its section "20 Top Experiences in Tibet".

Pilgrimage around Mount Kailash, Tibet. Heli Grauberg, 2016

On the way to the foot of Mount Kailash, Charan Sparsh, Tibet. Heli Grauberg, 2019

Full Tibetan prostration around Mount Kailash, Tibet.

Horse carrying pilgrims resting, Tibet.

2x Heli Grauberg, 2016

Kailash *inner kora,* or inner circle

The road of the inner kora runs close to Mount Kailash and is about 34 kilometres long. The route on the southern slope goes through a gorge, as if into a great natural amphitheatre, and then turns back again later. It is not a circuit around the sacred mountain, but goes around Mount Nandi, an outlier of Mount Kailash. Finishing the inner circle is one of the holiest pilgrimages. The road is so sacral that there is a saying: whoever has passed twelve Kailash 52-kilometre outer circles is qualified for the inner circle. This rule can only be broken if the outer kora, was completed in the Year of the Horse in the Chinese calendar (the last one was 2014, and the next will be 2026) because of the belief that this time is equal to twelve circles. In reality, there are no such rules, and everyone is free to do as they please, but there is also the saying that not fulfilling this precondition may have karmic consequences.

The websites of travel agencies promoting the inside circle say that the trek requires some mountaineering skills and equipment (provided by the tour company) and good physical fitness. There are no yaks and no horse and porter services on the inner trails.

The road begins in the Darchen village. Over approximately 34 kilometres, you pass Ashtapad, Nandi Parvat, Atmalingam, the Cave of Saptarish and Kuber Kunda, but the route can vary (sometimes you go to only one of the aforementioned places and then go straight to Darchen). The entire inner circle, or *inner kora,* runs along a rocky, snowy, icy and crevasse-rich path in the highlands, where there is no habitation. Only two small monasteries and a few stray dogs remain in the Sacred Circle area.

Every season, you can find a plethora of advertisements on the Internet advertising the inner circle of the Kailash pilgrimage, mainly provided by Nepali travel agencies. Unfortunately, the inner *kora* has been closed to foreigners for several years now. Chinese officials say they closed the area after an alleged great loss of life near Saptarishi Cave. Nevertheless, I haven't found any proof of what exactly happened. The e-book *Kailash with Mohanji: The Inner Kora* reported that a group of inner kora pilgrims were refused permission from China to enter the area due to the death of about 25 people near the Saptarishi Cave. The group did manage to take a couple of other inner trails. The leader of the group, Guru Mohanji, has one other sad message to tell his fellow travellers in the book: the ancient holy wise yogis, or *rishis,* who live in the cave and are invisible to our eyes, are disappointed in humans (he is said to have contacted them). More and more pilgrims are not visiting the place on spiritual grounds, and they don't show any kind of respect. Sometimes they come to photograph themselves next to a 6000-

metre-high cave and leave empty beer cans and other garbage around it. This place is very, very sacred in the world and, according to Guru Mohanji's theory, *rishis* push away these inappropriate vibrations, which can cause people to have sudden heart attacks or death from other dramatic causes. Who knows, maybe Guru Mohanji is right…

I have also dreamed of doing the whole inner circle and have contacted the Tibetan tourist office several times. The last answer I got was in the summer of 2018: "Unfortunately, the *inner kora* of Kailash is still closed to foreigners and could stay so from five to ten years." The theory from the book about the deaths in the inner circle reached me in 2019.

Knowing how Chinese laws and regulations can change in the blink of an eye, devout foreigners are still left with some small hope to visit this sacred region one day.

Saptarishi Cave *(Serdung Chuksum)* is one of the hardest challenges for those who take on the Mount Kailash inner circle. It means a 90-degree rise to the mountain on slippery open rocks, and climbing Saptarishi Cave, which is essentially a balcony with 13 little stupas *(chörtens)*, and all this in high altitude conditions (6000 m above sea level). The platform in front of the cave, which resembles a natural balcony, is only two metres wide and about 40 metres long. The balcony, lined with coloured streamers, is home to 13 smaller stupas. From this balcony, there is a very special view straight down into the valley, with the blue-green Lake Rakshastal in the background.

Some beliefs say that *siddha* Agastya also lives in this cave – one of the most famous holy men in all of India, who passes on knowledge straight from Shiva. It is also said that contact with Agastya is always made through consciousness and, for this reason, you don't really have to find his location and drag your physical body anywhere.

Saptarishi Cave is home to many ancient Indian wise men, or *rishis,* and the belief goes that the Hindu god Shiva composed 100 verses there in praise of his consort, the goddess Parvati. The cave, with 13 stupas, is maintained by a few inhabitants of the local monastery. According to Tibetan tradition, the walls are painted red, and pilgrims who have managed to drag themselves to the cave place their personal belongings in a special place to be blessed by the god Shiva. There are also supposed to be some religious books there to have a look at. Once the pilgrim has managed to climb up the 90-degree hill and propel himself onto the two-metre-wide balcony lined with stupas and prayer flags, it is surely the best time to gather strength for the future and to seize the special moment for spiritual practices. *Om Namah Shivaya… Om Mani Padme Hum…*

Thank you sincerely Dmitry Zadernovskiy for the pictures of the inner kora!

2x Kailash inner kora, Saptarishi Cave on the mountain side and 13 Chörtens (Thirteen stupas).

In translation, *Ashtapad* means eight steps. Eight steps to enlightenment, a mountain range with eight peaks… However, Jains also call Mount Kailash itself Ashtapad. There are so many stories and legends related to Ashtapad that you never know what it really is and where it's located…

The Jain scriptures say that the first Jain Tirthankar, Bhagwan, attained *nirvana*—a state of complete knowledge, peace and liberation that breaks the chain of rebirths—at Ashtapad Tirth. His son, King Chakravarti Bharat (the first universal emperor of the Jains), built a beautiful palace of precious stones, with eight steps leading up to it, as a memorial to the place of nirvana. To date, no one has actually been able to confirm the exact location of Ashtapad, which is why it is considered to be a "lost" Tirth.

For Jainists, Ashtapad also symbolizes the eight steps to enlightenment, each step representing one petal of an eight-petalled lotus flower. Near Mount Kailash, on the other hand, there are eight valleys, all of which lead pilgrims straight to the Centre of the Universe – the heart of the holy mountain. Many saints are known to meditate in the so-called Ashtapad caves, which are isolated from human habitation. From there, one can enjoy a magnificent view of Nandi and the southern slopes of Mount Kailash, where a kind of spine (Meru Danda) runs through the centre of the mountain.

Mount Nandi is located very close to Mount Kailash and fills an important role. When the god Shiva is in deep meditation on Mount Kailash and can't always hear the prayers of the pilgrims, Nandi takes on the role of a messenger and gets everybody's wishes, prayers and messages to Shiva. *Nandi Parvat*, the sacred bull Nandi, is Shiva's transportation and symbolizes strength and ignorance.

Kailash inner kora, Saptarishi Cave on the mountain side.

South side of Mount Kailash, inner circle (inner kora).
4x Dmitry Zadernovskiy, 2019

What is a pilgrimage?

Pilgrimage is one of the oldest spiritual traditions and means a journey to a sacred place. It can be physically demanding. In some cases, the journey is meaningless and the only thing that matters is the destination. There is a saying that visiting a sacred place gives the pilgrim some of the power hidden in that place. Different religions have different destinations: Hindus go to the Ganges, Muslims to Mecca, Catholics to Rome or to Portugal, to the village of Fátima. To each their own.

The pilgrimage journey gives you the opportunity to take a break from your busy lifestyle and look within yourself. It could also serve as a challenge to take on a big adventure and to meet new people. Some pilgrimage places are old and ancient; some are rather new. Some are attained through great suffering; some are reached very easily.

Some people are looking for inspiration from the pilgrimage; others don't really know why they started the journey. Some just follow their instincts. Some await great blessings from sacred places, for the power of God to be transferred to them. Pilgrimage can be a life-changing experience, where the pilgrim lets everything old go and is open to everything good and new. It's time to focus what is really important and to notice more than ever the gifts given to us by life.

There have been times when I have consciously gone to pilgrimage sites, and there have been times when I came upon them by chance. I have happened to cross the pilgrimage roads in Varanasi, Haridwar, Rishikesh and Rudraprayag. I've been to the Christian monastery of Taizé in France; Lumbini, the Buddhist sacred pilgrimage places in Nepal; Fatima, the Catholic mecca in Portugal; and ancient Stonehenge in England – the solstice night with my back against a giant boulder was also a time of pilgrimage and introspection for me.

Once, during a trip to Bangladesh in the sweltering heat, I caught a true classic cold – a very high fever, a terrible runny nose and a tiring cough – as a result of getting drenched and caught in a draught. That was before COVID-19, so I could visit the landmarks of the capital, Dhaka, even when sick. Though sick, we entered Bangladesh's most important Hindu temple, the Dhakeshwari Mandir, where I bought a freshly carved half-metre statue of Saraswati, the goddess of knowledge, art and music. We headed further behind the gate of the Muslim mosque to take some photos, when suddenly, a henna red-haired man invited us inside. I quickly pulled a thin shawl around my head, and there I was, the only female, standing in the mosaic-adorned Star Mosque, amidst amazed Muslim men praying. We also visited a couple of centuries-old authentic Armenian church belonging to the Armenian community of Dhaka, and when I got up the next morning, there was no sign of the annoying and severe cold that had just set in. A miraculous healing with the help of the shrines?

Despite the religious nature of the place, I was just being with myself and sending good prayers and wishes. You don't have to be a religious to go on a pilgrimage.

Ganga Aarti ceremony held every night by Ganges, Varanasi, India. Heli Grauberg, 2012

The Sri Ranganatha (or Lord Vishnu) Temple.
Skanda Vale Ashram was established by Guru Sri Subramanium in 1973 as a place of pilgrimage for people of different faiths to serve and worship together harmoniously. Wales, UK.

Photo by Skanda Vale

Celebration of the summer solstice in the Stonehenge stone circle (Shakti Sings Choir), Wiltshire, England.

Heli Grauberg, 2018

Just before the Hindu temple was inaugurated (statues still blindfolded). Sri Saraswathi Mantapam, Sharavana Baba ashram, Kerala, India.

Heli Grauberg, 2013

Monasteries around Mount Kailash

There are five monasteries near Mount Kailash: Choku (also called Nyari), Dirapuk, Zutulpuk, Selung (Serlung Gompa) and Gyangzha (Gyangdrag). Selung and Gyangzha are located in the area of the inner circle, or inner *kora*, and the other three are on the road of the outer *kora*, or outer circle.

Choku monastery (4,875 metres above sea level) was built in the 13th century and is first on the road of the outer circle pilgrims. You only have to look up to notice the sacred place built high up on the mountainside. The monastery's Choku statue, seashell and teapot are accompanied by a mystical legend. In the 17th century, an army invading the monastery tried to grab those three items to take with them, but the gods used their mystical power to prohibit the villainous act: the statue suddenly became so heavy that the soldiers could not carry it anymore and left it by the river. The seashell magically flew back to the sanctuary and the tea in the teapot turned into blood. The invaders were thus left with nothing.

Taking photos in the monastery is strictly forbidden, with good reason. In 1991, a group of people from Nepal stole 16 ancient statues at the request of Western art dealers. Two of the arrested thieves confessed that they had used photographs taken earlier by tourists to devise their plan to steal the statues.

Outer circle pilgrims can stay their first night at the guesthouse of the Dirapuk (Drirapuk) monastery (approx. 5000 m above sea level). *Drirapuk* translated from Tibetan means "the cave of the female yak horn". It's said that it was here, in the 13th century, that the renowned yogi Gyalwa Gotsangpa stayed and meditated for a long time. Drkukpa Publications, the website of the so-called red hats line of the Drukpas (aka Tibetan Buddhism), says that it was Gotsangpa who founded the tradition of the Mount Kailash pilgrimage and set the length of the journey – 52 kilometres. He also had the honour of discovering new Himalayan sacred places and caves that were very helpful to many yogis during their praxis and getting to enlightenment.

The monastery built on Gotsangpa Cave was fully destroyed during the Chinese Cultural Revolution. It was rebuilt in the 1980s and is now a popular destination among pilgrims.

The monastery's newer, simple guest house is available for pilgrims to stay in, according to the website, and also serves simple meals. Please note that the number of beds is limited, there are no showers and it's recommended that you bring your own sleeping bag. Accommodation information could change.

The monastery's doors are usually open all day and the adventurers are free to explore the sanctuary. In 2016, I stayed nearby in the guesthouse and visited the sanctuary. The dim and cool monastery, full of incense smoke, overlooked statues of Buddha, colourful Buddhist murals and Tibetan shawls, or *khata*, and the outside wall was lined with rows of white stupas.

Zutulpuk Monastery (4,800 metres above sea level) is almost at the end of the pilgrimage and is the last chance to rest on the pilgrimage circle before the third day. The surrounding natural scenery is magnificent, and according to Tibetan and Nepali tourist offices, the conditions of these accommodations are a bit better than those of the guesthouse owned by the Dirapuk monastery.

Selung (Sherlung gompa) Monastery (5000 meters above sea level) is the first one you notice on Kailash inner *kora*. It offers an amazing view from the south side of the sacred mountain and Mount Nandi. This monastery was built centuries ago for monks to meditate. Most of the sanctuary was destroyed during the Cultural Revolution but is now partially renovated and mainly used as a place of meditation and prayer for the inner circle pilgrims.

Gyangzha (Gyangdrag gompa) Monastery (5,075 meters above sea level) was the first monastery built in the region of Mount Kailash in the 13th century. It is one of the oldest and most important monasteries in Western Tibet. The sanctuary, located beside the roads of the inner circle, has been restored since the Cultural Revolution.

Dirapuk Monastery near Mount Kailash, Tibet.
                Heli Grauberg, 2016

Monastery of Choku, Tibet.

Monks on a pilgrimage around Mount Kailash, Tibet.

2x Heli Grauberg, 2019

Inspiring books by Russian doctor and scientist Ernst Muldashev

In Search of the City of God: In the Embrace of Shambala and *In the Search of the City of God: Golden Plates of Harati*

Ernst Muldashev (Ernst Muldašev), a famous Russian physician and scientist, doctor of medicine and professor, is the founder of a new branch of medicine: regenerative surgery, or growing human tissues. He is the first in the world to have successfully performed eye transplants and performs hundreds of highly complex operations every year. Not only is he the author of many books and a champion sportsman in sports tourism, he has also led scientific expeditions to Tibet, the Himalayas and Egypt, where, in addition to his specialty, he has studied everything to do with esotericism and religion.

After the Himalayan expedition, this medical doctor came up with the theory that Mount Kailash is actually a pyramid built by people of subtle energies in ancient times, surrounded by smaller pyramids and linked to Giza in Egypt and Teotihuacan in Mexico. With the help of numerous drawings made during the expedition, he proved that the peculiarly shaped mountains are, in fact, giant pyramids. Muldashev is convinced that he found the ancient city of Shambala, or the City of the Gods, during his expedition, and that the same Kailash complex is linked to our life on planet Earth.

On a trip with holy men, Muldashev came to understand that the ornaments and symbols of the Nepali temples originated near Mount Kailash, and that, allegedly, the people who did this live not only on the earth but also beneath it. The Kailash complex was modelled on the famous Khalachakra mandala, and is therefore able to have a strong and positive influence on people all over the world (mandalas are mystical images given to Earth by a higher consciousness). In Nepal, during a meeting between Muldashev and Astaman, a representative of the ancient family Bindacharaya (keepers of the Harat, or protectors of the cave), it was revealed that there is a statue of the Reading Man near Kailash, which is usually impossible to see because it is always surrounded by clouds. The figure was supposed to attract clouds and no one was allowed to go there—whoever approached would die. The Reading Man symbolizes ancient superior knowledge that is written on the golden plates he is holding. During the conversation with Astaman, Muldashev couldn't even imagine that he would be in Tibet when the clouds would fade and he would see the mysterious figure of the Reading Person. He even managed to get a picture of it.

Astaman also told Muldashev about a legend of the subterranean world of Kailash that has three entrances and is completely impossible to get into, because the forces acting there will make a person age instantaneously. There's also a plain on the mountain where only gods are allowed.

There is a mirror on the northern side of Kailash that shadows people with dark forces. It is said that Kailash has enchanted this place and created a Valley of Death, also known as the Mirror of the Ruler of Death, Yama. You always go alone to the valley. Concentrated time will evaluate the person and decide whether to kill them or let them live on. The maximum time one can spend before the mirror is five minutes; after that, the ruler of Death will do their job. Nearby, you can find two reddish stone chips reminiscent of four-eyed dogs. You have to lie between them, close your eyes and be in front of your own conscience – the jury of the Ruler of Death – Yama. It's a mirror where the whole past and conscience of the pilgrim is evaluated by the unknown energetic intellect.

Muldashev did manage to find these doglike red stones and stand in front of the Yama's court. Vivid images from his life started to pass before his eyes. His heart reacted to every frame with sweet satisfaction or dissatisfaction. And at that moment before Yama, he realised that it is not the person's deeds, but their thoughts, which are most important in their lives. He also understood that he had been put on this earth to listen to his intuition. Between the stones, Muldashev was given the knowledge that he had wasted a lot of time in his life, especially in his youth. His consciousness was nagging him about not listening to his intuition, and, of course, about his wasted time. What would be the punishment of Yama? Yama did not take Muldashev to him and did not make him an oldster; the punishment was an unbearable pain in the stomach area. The pain did not come from the stomach, but from the soul, flowing into his stomach. Muldashev acknowledged that negative energy was flowing out, followed by a terrible stomach pain. His soul was being cleansed through pain; that was his punishment for time wasted…

There is a place called The Hungry Devil's Place, not very far from Mount Kailash, which can also only be visited alone, because even a friend can betray you and perish there. The Hungry Devil turns evil thoughts into reality, and one can imagine what these thoughts mean: you might fight with an invisible enemy, go crazy, scream and run and finally, being very tired, you ask the Hungry Devil to make your body a stone. "It's a very sacred place and also very, very dangerous. Don't go there," Lama Khetsun Zangpo told Muldashev. After some time, however, the man managed to find the place and, standing alone on the top of the hill, again suffering from a terrible stomachache, he looked in the direction of the Hungry Devil. He heard, as if he were being told: "Go away from here!" And he did.

Muldashev says: "For some reason people think they can explain everything because they know all, and this know-it-all mentality has brought humanity to absurdities, like an archaeological explanation of building the pyramids, according to which pyramids were built before inventing the wheel, by half-wild slaves. People are so in love with themselves, so absorbed by the sin of believing themselves to be gods, that they cannot just accept the belief where the inexplicable really does exist in the world and where the human really is not God, but just a result of a divine experiment. But how we would love to think of ourselves as Gods or at least omniscient!"

Pyramid shaped mountains around Mount Kailash, Tibet. Heli Grauberg, 2016

One of the symbols of Tibetan Buddhism - the Golden Vajra at Swayambhunath Temple. According to legend, ancient people used this machine to build mountains with thought energy (according to ancient Tibetan texts), Kathmandu, Nepal.
Heli Grauberg, 2011

Buddha Park, Kathmandu, Nepal.
Heli Grauberg, 2019

Tibetan mantra on the rocks around Mount Kailash, Tibet. Heli Grauberg, 2016

The incredible story of Tracey Alysson

It was in 2006 when Tracey Alysson began a special pilgrimage to Mount Kailash. She knew neither the local language nor culture, she did not have any previous contact with the highlands and she didn't have the slightest idea how to do this pilgrimage. It was an invitation from the higher realms, the Tibetan spiritual beings called *dakinis,* who are self-manifesting beings of love. The sacred mountain called her. The kora around Mount Kailash was supposed to be done only in the way dedicated pilgrims do it in Tibet—in full prostration: you have to lay down on your face at full length, stand up and lay down again where your hands reached.

A Tibetan religious practice, prostration (bowing) cuts through a human's ego and arrogance and removes obstacles from their spiritual path. This deed is done to show respect to Buddha, Dharma (study) and Sangha (community). Your mind, body and heart are cleansed. Prostration can also be practised by standing in one place, the way Tibetans do at home by the altar or, for example, before entering the sanctuary.

Prostration is a Tibetan religious practice in which one holds their hands in prayer above their head, then hands are placed on the forehead, then the throat and, finally, the heart. The next step is to fall on one's knees, followed by lying down fully extended, hands stretched forth. Then we rise back onto our knees and stand up, and everything begins again from the exact spot your hands reached. Experiencing this as one long prayer…

Covering 52 kilometres this way could take weeks, if not a month. When she was making her plans, Tracey did not know that she was the first Western person to try this kind of pilgrimage.

In frosty winds, snow, and rain, it took the American 28 days to finish the kora: five to nine hours a day on her face, stretching out and standing up again. She wore a special leather apron and pads for her knees and hands made by a friend. She repeated the holy syllables, or mantras. She did this through dust, sand, dirt, yak and horse dung, burning sun, rain and snow. With every prostration, her forehead was smeared with sacred dust and dirt. Braving cold and wind in harsh highland conditions, living in a tent (with helpers around), without basic washing facilities or toilets.

For much of the time, she struggled with flu, diarrhoea and high-altitude sickness. On her journey, she met curious people and friendly wandering dogs. She experienced weird local habits where strangers entered her tent without asking permission and wandered around. She also bowed through the Tibetan hillside graveyard used by Tibetans for the Sky burial (see the section on the Sky burial). She passed, or, more accurately, almost crawled, the 52-kilometre circle alone, always having to save her energy for the evening to find helpers and a place to camp. Every moment in Tibet – feeling cold, pain, nausea or comfort – was to be filled with pure joy from that moment on. Tibet let her forget her obstacles and excuses… When she returned from the pilgrimage, where she had made all her own choices and taken all the risks, Tracey said that she finally knew and felt who she really was. After the pilgrimage, she felt more mature, more open, conscious, loving, confident and humble, and she felt that she was a much better person.

Extracts from Tracey Alysson's book (chosen by Alysson at my request):

"We all have obstacles that make us believe that love is not available to us. This book (this korah/pilgrimage) is about my obstacles, and about my journey through them to love's open arms, devouring, digesting, and purifying me so that my availability to receive love is all that is left…"

"It has taken me a long time to realize that the issue about Kailash is not about me. I thought it would change me, destroy me, and devour me. It did, but that was not what was important. Kailash is a door that keeps opening. It was stepping into the door that was important. It is also important to realize that it was not my door. I stepped into the door, on the door's terms. To do so, I had to leave my terms behind. I had to leave knowing behind. I had to step into space knowing in my deepest heart that the wings of love would keep me from crashing on the rocks, and would steer me because I had entered a plane where I no longer knew…"

"Even though receiving the next level of truth in my body and mind as well as my spirit feels like a dying, and it is on one level, maybe it is better said that in fact the deadness begins to be cut away. My beliefs about my history, my childhood, that is, my attachments, are like parasites, sucking my life energy, making me more and more rigid. Cutting away the necrosis lets life have what belongs to it: its own energies."

"I have been immeasurably blessed by Kailash. Kailash brought together my body and spirit, my density and ecstasy. It brought me home to the spiritual universe that I am, residing in this human body and personality. Now it is the joyfulpainful work to live out in the fibers of all the levels of my being the truth that compassion is infinite, and that

infinite compassion is right here with me, every moment, just waiting for me to trust it. I spread my wings into life. Winds of Kailash, carry me!"

Tracey Alysson, PhD, a practicing clinical psychologist, has put her special and inspiring pilgrimage into a book, *Dying & Living in the Arms of Love: One Woman's Journey around Mount Kailash.*

Tracey Alysson's last prostration of the pilgrimage, 2006. Tarboche (Yama Dwar), where Tibetans hold religious festivals.

My sincere thanks to Tracey Alysson who sent this picture for inclusion in the book.

Prices

You can get to Mount Kailash through Nepal or fly straight to Tibet and begin your pilgrimage (the border points are Lipulekh Pass in Uttarakhand and Nathu La in Sikkim—in addition to some other choices for Indian pilgrims).

The high season for kora is from May to October. That said, many tourist offices don't add October to their plans anymore, because the temperature drops considerably. Companies organise the clients' Chinese visas, permits to enter the mountain region and other necessary equipment, because lone travellers are not permitted to go to Kailash anymore – at least not from Nepal. Coming from the Nepal side and going overland, through the Rasuwagadhi-Kerung border crossing, the price of the Kathmandu Holiday Tours and Travels outer kora package I chose was US$2,290 in 2019. By plane and helicopter from Nepal almost to the Tibetan border (with a bus in Tibet), the entire Kailash pilgrimage package cost US$3,150 (including the outer circle). This price included a small excursion in the Nepali capital Kathmandu, three nights in a decent hotel in Kathmandu, all accommodations during the trip (rather basic ones), bus transportation, tour guides, jacket and travel bags as a gift from the tourist office, permits to enter the mountain region, Chinese visa, all catering throughout the trip (they had their own chefs with vegetarian food and Indian cuisine), unlimited drinking water and medicine for mountain sickness. All the pilgrims had to cover was travel insurance and plane tickets to Kathmandu and back home, Nepali visa at the border, the cost of extra nights at the Kathmandu hotel if necessary and, if you wish, a horse or porter fee on the mountain (they can be quite pricey) and tips for the servicing personnel.

The inner kora package, starting from Nepal by land to Tibet, cost US$2,900 in 2019 and included, in addition to all of the above, helmets and other mountaineering equipment and trained assistants. The numbers above were fairly average prices for pilgrimage packages offered by Nepalese travel agencies to foreigners in 2019 (prices for pilgrims from India are usually significantly cheaper).

To guarantee a place in the group, I had to pay a booking fee of US$300. Not every tourist office has such cheap advance pay conditions, and quite often, almost the whole package price has to be paid in instalments before the pilgrimage begins. The booking fee was paid to the representative of the tour company in Kathmandu via Western Union and the rest could be paid in cash on the spot just before the pilgrimage. A copy of the passport and a digital photo of other documents also had to be e-mailed to the travel company. From then on, all one could do was wait.

The permit to enter the Mount Kailash region was sent to me via e-mail approximately two weeks before the pilgrimage began (time varies and it's hard to tell when the permit is given). After getting the permits, you can feel a bit more at ease about the trip. Chinese visas are made on the spot and this is why you have to get to Nepal three or four days before the pilgrimage package actually begins. Travelers from India get the visa in India.

Those who head out on the pilgrimage to Kailash from Nepal are usually from India, and groups can be very big – around 40-60 people (groups are smaller for the inner kora), and you rarely meet other foreigners. A lone Western person, especially when they happen to be blond, can invite lots of attention from travel companions (I experienced this during my air travels in different pilgrim stops). The group I finally had to join on my first pilgrimage was small and consisted mostly of Indian businessmen who travelled to Kailash frequently (some even every year), and luckily, my presence did not excite them at all. On my other trip I had my good friend Maria with me and made friends with some of the Nepali and Indian members of the the group. Many Tibetan tourism companies are rather specialized in servicing Western people.

The choice is the pilgrim's to make.

Locals working.
Tibetan mantra on the rocks surrounding Mount Kailash, Tibet.

Friends on Kailash pilgrimage, Tibet.

Young yak close to Mount Kailash, Tibet.
Photos by Heli Grauberg, 2016

What to pack

- Waterproof camping boots – if you go on the pilgrimage through Nepal, you can find some boots and other camping equipment in Kathmandu for a very good price;
- travel stick and an oxygen tank – you can buy this straight from the Darchen village near Kailash;
- windproof jacket – Nepali tour companies often give their logoed jackets to their groups as a gift, so you should ask about it before buying one;
- plastic trousers and a rain cape – only when it's raining. I did not need mine on my first trip, but they came in handy on the second journey;
- lighter athletic shoes;
- hat, gloves, scarf, socks, warm jumper, hiking pants, leggings;
- tunic, also formal (for women) – as there is often no toilet, it is especially good for women to bring longer blouses. Also, more formal attire if the group is organising ceremonies. A dress or something comfortable if you are going to Lake Manasarovar to get wet – it is not appropriate for women to wear a swimsuit, but it is for men to wear swimming trunks;
- a small shoulder bag – if you hire a porter to carry your backpack, you can store your phone, money, notebook, pencil and other essentials;
- empty water bottle – you can refill this repeatedly. And if you wish, you can use empty light bottles for holy water (for example, from Lake Manasarovar, Gauri Kund, Charan Sparsh and other holy places). Take a waterproof marker to write on the bottle where the water is from;
- thermos – if you wish to carry a hot beverage with you;
- additional phone – for local Chinese and Nepali pre-paid cards (if you don't have a device with multiple SIM-slots);
- big plastic trash bag – to protect your travel bag from rain, if it's being transported on the bus roof, for example;
- Nepali plug – if the travel is through Nepal;
- Chinese plug;

- flashlight – I recommend taking an extra battery, because you need a flashlight quite often. It's good to have a head lamp, which will be especially useful when going to the toilet or brushing your teeth when it's dark.
- battery bank – sometimes the electricity in the guesthouse was absent, so this was a way to keep my camera and phone going;
- sunglasses – I recommend placing them in a bag with a rope wrapped around it so they can hang around your neck;
- notebook and pencil;
- small lock for your bag – we left our bags in Darchen village hotel for some days. Just to be safe, it's better to buy a little lock;
- small mirror;
- small scissors;
- personal hygiene products;
- bigger towel – for everyday use and to sit on after swimming in Lake Manasarovar;
- pillowcase – good to use in more ascetic guesthouses;
- toilet paper – a necessity;
- hand sanitiser;
- tablets for mountain sickness – before you buy them, you should check to see if the tour company provides them;
- band-aids, painkillers, diarrhoea tablets;
- sun cream with UV protection;
- herpes cream – in case of an unexpected flare-up;
- chocolate, raisins, peanuts – they advise sweets in high altitudes for an energy boost;
- if you wish, some gifts for locals and children – they especially like sweets and all kinds of foreign gadgets: felt-tips, stickers, notebooks, sunglasses, etc;
- photos of your loved ones – someone to share your pilgrimage with (very popular among Hindus).

If your trip to Tibet through Nepal falls during a monsoon period, it's useful to get yourself some waterproof shoes and an umbrella.

Local Simikot village women carrying pilgrims' bags, Nepal.

Mount Kailash, Tibet.
2× Heli Grauberg, 2016

Mountain sickness

When going to Mount Kailash, you have to be really attentive to your health, because this kind of altitude can inflict many health problems and even endanger your life. It's recommended to do adequate physical training before this kind of trip—by practicing yoga, for example. You can ask for a health check from your family doctor and can get vaccinated against certain illnesses. It's a good idea to visit a dentist because toothache is supposedly made worse under changing pressure conditions. The Nepali travel company asked for health certificates from those going on the Kailash pilgrimage. My family doctor did not wish to give out this kind of document (probably didn't want to risk liability if something were to happen to me in Tibet) and suggested I pay some other doctor, who would organize a full check-up. I did not rush to pay for the certificate, and luckily there was no problem with the tourism company because of the missing health certificate.

Typical symptoms of mountain sickness are headache, tiredness and weakness, nausea and vomiting, loss of appetite, shortness of breath and sleep problems. To cure the person from mountain sickness, you have to get them down fast. Even getting them a few hundred metres lower will help the condition tremendously.

To prevent mountain sickness, I got some Diamox tablets (half a tablet a day) from my Nepali travel consultant and committed to drinking as much liquid I could. When travelling around the mountain, I always had an oxygen tank in my backpack, just in case I needed some extra oxygen. You can buy them rather cheap in Darchen. Approaching Mount Kailash by road is supposed to allow considerably more time for acclimatisation than by air. I was forced to travel to the mountain by plane and helicopter in 2016, in accordance with Chinese policies. To some, it makes no difference whether they approach Kailash by air or by road, but everyone is different. During both journeys, I suffered a few headaches, and serious sleep problems accompanied me during the whole 2019 pilgrimage.

I saw many pilgrims suffering from mountain sickness. I also learned in secret from the guides and Sherpas that during the last days of our first pilgrimage, six people had lost their lives in the area – all due to mountain sickness.

But mountain sickness isn't the only thing that can take a person's life in those high Tibetan plains… Just before going on pilgrimage in 2016, I met my former Hindu yoga teacher, Ashwin, on a yoga retreat at Yogiraj Gurunath Siddhanath. He was my first teacher in London, whose exciting two-hour Saturday morning yoga lessons were held in adjoining rooms at a real Hindu, or Murugan Temple, where services took place above our heads. He charged for a nominal fee 2£ (presumably because people often don't appreciate what they get for free). Himself a lawyer by profession, Ashwin did this all because of his kind heart and deep dedication. On the retreat, he heard about my plan to go to Mount Kailash and told me that his mother's doctor friend – a woman in her sixties and a very good family friend – had begun the same journey but did not return. She successfully finished the kora circle and, sitting in her car after the pilgrimage, preparing to drive back, she asked her companions for something to drink and then left this earth for heavenly realms. She had no health complaints whatsoever; perhaps it was just her "time to go". What better place and blessing could a dedicated Hindu soul ask to depart from one's body?

Evening sun setting on Mount Kailash, Tibet. Heli Grauberg, 2016

Pilgrims in Lake Manasarovar, Tibet. Heli Grauberg, 2016

Sherpas

Sherpas are members of a Nepali and Middle-Asian ethnic group who have lived for centuries in the Himalayas and have developed a capacity to survive under the highland's thin air and low oxygen levels. Oxygen deficiency affects the lungs and the brain and, of course, the whole organism. According to scientific studies, Sherpas have highly developed mechanisms for transporting oxygen to the tissues and have been genetically adapted to high altitude conditions since ancient times. They also tend not to get mountain sickness because their haemoglobin levels are lower than average.

Before their world fame in mountaineering, Sherpas were nomadic herders, farmers, weavers and salt traders. Their culture and economy changed dramatically in the 20th century, when Everest became a favourite destination for mountaineers. Without the Sherpas, many travelers would not have been able to survive in the high mountains. Their resilience is admirable, and they are the source of most of the guides on the slopes of the world's highest peak, Mount Everest, as well as in the Kailash region. In the thin air, where it is difficult for the average person to move with a backpack, Sherpas run around under a load like tiny mountain goats. They are experts at helping mountaineers: they know the area well, carry heavy equipment, repair climbers' ladders and ropes, stand in for the guides, and cook. Sherpas are generally very friendly, but not intrusive. Their job is a very risky one, and getting home from work is not always guaranteed. Almost every Sherpa visits a local sanctuary before the Everest trip and asks God for protection. According to *Outside* magazine, the chances of a Sherpa dying while climbing the world's highest mountain are significantly higher than for US soldiers in wars or miners in mines. A Sherpa's work is quite well paid compared to other Nepali occupations. At the peak of Everest's climb, a lead Sherpa's three-month pay can reach nearly US$6,000 (*The Washington Post*, 2014). Sums so big offer the opportunity in poor Nepal to save some money and create your own company, which many former Sherpas have done.

Sherpas, Nepal. Shutterstock, Zzvet

INTERESTING FACTS ABOUT NEPAL

Nepal

Namaste! That's the greeting with which the Nepali people, hands clasped at the chest, greet you and send you on your way. The Sanskrit word *namaste* is used to pass on respect and means: "I greet the God in you." In yoga, this position is known as *pranamasana,* or prayer position, where attention is focused inward.

Nepal is a land of tourists, mountains and mountaineering. The land of the world's highest mountain, Mount Everest (Jomolungma), monasteries, rituals and mantras. Eight of the world's 8000-metre-high mountains are located in this country.

Buddha's birthland, Nepal, is a country between China and India which lies at the foot of the Himalayas and is inhabited by over 30 million people. According to its constitution, Nepal was a Hindu kingdom until the parliament lost this provision in 2006. Until that point, it had been the world's only Hindu country. According to Wikipedia, around 81.3% of the population in Buddha's birthland are Hindus; they are followed by Buddhists (9%), Muslims (4.4%) and some smaller religious groups. It's rather common in Nepal for Buddhists to visit Hindu temples and Hindus to visit Buddhist sanctuaries.

According to legend, Prince Siddharta Gautama, who later became the enlightened Buddha, was born in Nepal. The entire temple complex in Lumbini, the birthplace of Buddha, is protected by its designation as a UNESCO World Heritage Site, and every year, thousands of Buddhists and ordinary tourists make the pilgrimage there.

There is a saying that Nepal has five seasons: spring, summer, rainy period, autumn and winter. Spring in Nepal is a time for the beautiful national flower, rhododendron, to bloom. The daily summer rains can be annoying, but they are followed by a freshness and by beautiful views of Nepali skies and magnificent white Himalayan peaks. Winter days are sunny and warm, but nights can surprise you with a crisp cold. The main tourism seasons are in spring from March to May and in autumn from September to November, but the country is worth visiting all year round.

Namaste! A Nepali man bestowing a greeting. Shutterstock, T. Tarras

At a café next to the Boudhanath stupa, we had vegetable-stuffed and steamed momos (comes with different fillings), Nepal.
Heli Grauberg, 2019

Moments of thought under the Buddhist praying flags in Buddha's birthplace, Lumbini, Nepal.
Heli Grauberg, 2011

The Capital: Kathmandu

Nepal is a poor country, and its capital, Kathmandu, sits at the top of the list of the world's most affordable cities. Smelling of incense, its dusty and narrow streets are full of people, cars, motorcycles, rickshaws, temples, dogs and businesses.

Western-like Thamel, with its hotels, bars, shops and travel agencies, is the tourist district in Kathmandu. Luckily, the locals are not as intrusive with their offers as are their neighbours, Indian merchants, in their own land. The city is full of travel agencies, because the country is also full of interesting and exotic places: there are trips to Buddha's birthplace, Lumbini, and Nepal's old capital, Bhaktapur. There are national parks, nature preserves, and opportunities for rafting, kayaking… even going on safari. Or a trip to the world's highest mountain, Mount Everest, or Annapurna. Why not a pilgrimage to Mount Kailash?

During the trekking season, or the season of long, hard walks, the small shops on Thamel's main street are packed with foreigners who find hiking clothes, boots, sleeping bags and all sorts of other hiking gear at great prices. In the evenings, bars, restaurants and clubs, sometimes with a Western flair, are packed with tourists and locals. You can buy a European-style alcoholic cocktail, an Italian pizza, or a burger, or you can have some authentic Nepali ethnic cuisine. There is a dazzling array of options.

View on a Kathmandu street, Nepal.
Heli Grauberg, 2008

Relaxing dogs in the capital, Nepal.

Souvenir shop, Kathmandu, Nepal.

2x Heli Grauberg, 2019

The Goddess Kumari

Nepal is an interesting country where not only dead, but living goddesses, or *kumaris,* are worshipped. You can check the goddess out yourself when on Durbar Square in Kathmandu; just find the Kumari Ghar house. Sometimes she looks out of the window, but it's hard to predict when she will do so. There are a lot of tourists, hoping to see her in her window. She is always dressed in red, decorated with jewellery and heavy eye makeup, with a third eye on her forehead. The word *kumari* comes from the ancient Sanskrit word *Kaumarya,* which means virgin (also young girl, princess). Kumari is thought to be an incarnation of the goddess Taleju. Goddesses are chosen from among children who range in age from three to five years and whose horoscopes match. Strict rules apply to their looks: the girl's neck has to be as a seashell, in addition, she must have a body shaped like a fig, eyelashes as long as a cow's, calves as pretty as a deer's and a chest like that of a lion. Her eyes and hair must be as black as charcoal, she must have 20 teeth in her mouth, and there are some other requirements. For a candidate to be chosen, she must pass a tough test during a Hindi festival. One hundred and eight buffaloes and goats are sacrificed in the garden of the Taleju temple in honour of the goddess Kali, and the candidates are brought in the candlelight to see their severed heads and dancing men in masks. If that doesn't scare them, then in what is almost the final part of the test, the girl has to spend the night in the dark in the Taleju temple, surrounded by bloodied animal heads. And if that doesn't scare her, it's almost certain that the goddess has been chosen. Kumari symbolises serenity.

And then there is the last test. A variety of items are laid before the girl and she has to recognize things among them that belonged to the last Kumari. If the test is passed successfully, there is no doubt that the goddess has been correctly chosen. If all of the secret tantric cleaning rituals have been done with the help of the priests and the goddess has entered the child's body, the new living goddess Kumari can go to her new home in the Kathmandu city centre – Kumari Ghar temple palace. While being a goddess, she can leave the house only 13 times a year, accompanied, during celebrations, and she is always carried because her feet cannot touch the land. There are more *kumaris* in Nepal, but only the most important ones are isolated. Child goddesses are worshipped by both Buddhists and Hindus.

After the onset of puberty, meaning right after the first menstruation, goddesses have to go back to their old lives, which is not always easy. Having received their schooling only from private tutors, and with little contact with the outside world, these special children still have to continue their studies in public schools and start to interact with strangers and make close friends. Human rights activists in Nepal condemn the Kumari tradition, which robs children of their childhood and of the companionship of their parents and siblings.

The former royal Kumari, Rashmila Shakya (served in 1984 – 1991), writes in her autobiographic book *From Goddess to Mortal* that there are about a dozen chopped animal heads in the "scary room test," and this kind of ceremony is part of the royal Kumari's annual ritual, not just the final selection of *kumaris*. Also, the physical requirements are supposedly not that strict (*Global Press Journal*, 2012).

I am no exception – I also tried to catch a glimpse of the Kumari child goddess in the Kumari Ghar Temple Palace window during my trips to Nepal, but I haven't yet been so blessed.

Kumari at an Indra Jatra festival, 2017. Durbar Square, Nepal.
Shutterstock, Iryna Hromotska

Earthquake in 2015

On 25 April 2015, Nepal was hit by the worst earthquake in 80 years, measuring 7.8 on the Richter scale, followed by several aftershocks. The epicentre was located between the densely populated city of Kathmandu and Pokhara, some 80 kilometres from the capital. The death toll was estimated at between 8,500 and 9000, and around 22,000 people were injured. There was destruction across the country, and many were trapped under the rubble and lost their homes and businesses. Nearly 8 million Nepali people were affected in some way by the terrible event. Durbar Square, a UNESCO World Heritage site in the capital, with its beautiful temples and important historical buildings, was also badly affected.

Buddha's eyes crushed from the earthquake at the Swayambhunath temple complex.
Shutterstock, Thomas Dutour

Mount Everest, or Jomolungma

Nepal is a mountainous country, containing as many as eight of the world's highest mountains. Among others, you can see Mount Everest (Jomolungma), 60 million years old, with an impressive height of 8848 metres. This mountain was renamed in the 19th century honouring a British surveyor and geographer, Sir George Everest.

Everest lies in both Nepalese and Tibetan territory. The southern side of the mountain belongs to Nepal and the northern side to Chinese-occupied Tibet. However, most mountaineers prefer to approach the mountain via Nepal, as the route from there is a little friendlier in terms of nature, the tourism industry is more developed and there is no need to change travel plans because of unexpected Chinese border closures.

Visiting the roof of the world sounds ambitious, but this road is a game of life and death and is much dependent on luck. This is a place of overcoming yourself.

The first ones to reach the top of Everest, on 29th of May 1953, were a New Zealander, Edmund Hillary, and a Sherpa, Tenzing Norgay. Including stops at acclimatisation camps, it takes up to two months to reach the peak. The trekker usually needs extra oxygen to breathe, so the standard equipment for a mountaineering climb includes portable oxygen tanks, accompanied by local Sherpas and guides.

Hundreds of climbers go on this life-endangering road every year. Climbing the world's highest peak is many mountaineers' dream, but not everything goes as planned. Because of the lack of oxygen and the harsh weather conditions, hikers can get mountain sickness, fall, get caught in an avalanche or freeze to death. The slopes of Everest are littered with the frozen corpses of mountaineers. Often the bodies are not even removed from the base camps, because transport is almost impossible to organise and is terribly expensive. The corpses lie there as if someone had just died. Nowadays, landmarks have been put in place to let other mountaineers know where they are, and there have reportedly been around 200 of these unfortunate endings around the Mountain of Dreams. After the Nepali earthquake in 2015, Mount Everest was struck by an avalanche that hit a base camp and killed around 20 and injured more than 60 mountaineers. In this tragic year, nobody managed to climb to the peak. It was one of Mount Everest's most deadly accidents.

Life-threatening traffic jams at the summit of Everest, the world's highest mountain (Hillary Step - 8790 m above sea level, or death zone).

Sherpa Pasang Kaji PK took this picture of his companion, filmmaker Elia Saikaly, on his way to the top of Everest (fifth mountaineer on the right). Saikaly and PK were there as part of a documentary film crew capturing a group of Arab women conquering the mountain.

Photo by Pasang Kaji Sherpa, 2019

In May 2019, at the peak of the mountaineering season, a large mountain was suffering from overcrowding. In the so-called "death zone", at 8000 metres above sea level, where a person can only stay for a few minutes at best without an oxygen mask, queues of up to 12 hours had formed on the slopes full of trekkers (according to CNN, however, a few hundred people have visited the summit without supplementary oxygen over the years). The harsh weather conditions, lack of experience, depleted oxygen supplies and exhaustion led to the loss of 11 lives at the time.

The coveted Mount Everest has also been hit by a serious environmental problem that gave the mountain an infamous nickname – "world's highest junkyard". Mountaineers and their entourages produce so much waste during their two months on the road that they pose a risk of infection. The mountain is full of old camping equipment, broken tents, used oxygen tanks and huge piles of faeces, urine and refuse.

The government of Nepal made a decision that every team would pay a so-called "trash deposit" of US$4000 before going on the mountain. To get the money back, you have to return at least 8 kilograms of trash – oxygen tanks, urine and faeces excluded (*BBC News*, 2014).

Climbing the mountain is an expensive endeavour, with prices starting at US$35,000 and going up to US$90,000, according to *Adventure Alternative*. The price depends on whether you use Nepalese, Chinese or Western travel services, and on a number of additional factors. Following the tragic end of the 2019 season, stricter rules and higher prices have been introduced for those wishing to go on an Everest expedition.

A mountaineer crosses a crack in the glacier on his way to Everest.

Shutterstock, Zhosan Olexandr

Yeti

Is the yeti just folklore, or does it really exist? General opinion is that this large, hairy, two-legged, ape-like character lives in Nepal in the Himalayan mountains, but scientists think it is a myth. The first person to refer to the yeti was British colonel lieutenant Charles Howard-Bury in 1921. On an expedition to Jomolungma, he had allegedly seen a barefoot human footprint at 6400 meters. Later, there were photos taken high in Jomolungma of huge footprints, but scientists think they are deformed human footprints. Sir Edmund Hillary, the first to conquer Everest, and Sherpa Tenzing Norgay also saw large footprints up there. Even today, there are still a few people with a mythical belief in yetis, and some hikers still organise yeti expeditions in the Himalayas.

The small Nepali Khumjung village monastery is home to a specimen initially thought to be a yeti's scalp, which monks show people for a small fee. It's actually the same skull that Sir Edmund Hillary and journalist Desmond Doig brought back in the 1960s when they returned from an expedition seeking proof of the yetis.

Thought to be an amulet of good luck, the find was located in the home of a local witch in the village of Khumjung in Nepal and had belonged to the village for the past 240 years. It was not easy for the men investigating the existence of the yeti, Edmund Hillary and Desmond Doig, to take the half-football-shaped dome covered in hair to experts for identification. Eventually, with the help of financial donations and the involvement of the village mayor (a guard who travelled with the men to London), they were able to borrow the valuable find. However, the body part allegedly belonging to the yeti did not pass expert inspection and was simply identified as belonging to an animal (*The Guardian*, 1960).

Scalp at Khumjung Monastery, Nepal. This find, thought to be an amulet of good luck, used to be located in the village of Khumjung in Nepal, in the home of a local witch, and had belonged to the village for the last 240 years.
Shutterstock, Boyloso

Hippies

In the 1960s and 1970s, the capital of Nepal, Kathmandu, was a gathering point for young hippies and adventurers from Europe and America. Legal cannabis and marijuana were what brought the crowd in, but there was also the hope of mental enlightenment and the draw of just seeing the world. Kathmandu *Freak Street* was a hippie's Nirvana and was a direct bus ride away from the airport. This was all a sacred land to hippies— gods and marijuana.

They even had a bus line from London and Amsterdam to Nepal, but many came with cars and vans and motorcycles—some even by hitchhiking—through Turkey, Iran, Afghanistan, Pakistan and India. Some vehicles did not arrive at their destinations, neither did they come back; they were sold to locals in Nepal. The hippie movement died out toward the end of 1970s, when the Nepali government made the hippies' life miserable, implementing strict rules and threatening deportation, promising to send them straight back to India. Prohibiting cannabis played a huge role. The Iranian revolution at the end of the 1970s and Russia's invasion of Afghanistan, which closed the region's roads to Western tourists, also made passing the hippie road impossible. More than ten years of the hippie road had become history.

A dreamcatcher with mountains in the background.
Shutterstock, Marina Shin

Murder in the Royal household

On the first of June, 2001, Nepali citizens were shaken by the news of a murder committed by Prince Dipendra, an Eton student, while he was drunk and high on hashish. He shot randomly and killed his father, King Birendra, his mother, Queen Aishwarya, and some other members of the royal family, including his sister and brother. He wounded four more relatives and finally shot himself. According to the report, the floors of the palace were covered with large amounts of blood, brains, teeth and broken glass after the massacre.

In the beginning, they tried to hide the news, and the murder was presented as an accident. Prince Dipendra, who was in a coma, was made king. The special honour lasted for only three days, after which he died without ever regaining consciousness. Why he did what he did will probably always remain a mystery. According to one version, the crown prince, who had been educated in England, went into a fit of rage because his parents prohibited him from marrying the woman he had chosen. But many Nepalis are certain that it was a conspiracy to get rid of the royal family and that it was not really the king's son Dipendra who was behind the massacre.

Nepal was a kingdom from 1768 to 2008. Representatives of the Communist Party, aka Maoists, insisted on getting rid of the monarchy and dethroning the king, Gyanendra, who was the brother of Birendra. The Constituent Assembly of Nepal met in Kathmandu on 28 May 2008 and abolished royal power. The first president of Nepal elected by the parliament was Ram Baran Yadav, and the 2015 presidential election was won by a female candidate, Bidhya Devi Bhandari.

A statue of Nepal's King Birendra and Queen Aishwarya. Shutterstock, Siraj Ahmad

Caste system

Nepal's caste system is quite similar to the one in India. At the top is the highest caste of priests and teachers, the Brahmin caste, followed by the Chettri (governors and soldiers), the Vaisya (traders and farmers), the Sudra (artisans and unskilled labourers), and at the bottom of the hierarchy are the Dalit, or untouchables ("The Caste System in Nepal", Sociologi og Kulturanalyse, Syddansk Universitet, 2014).

In 1962, a law was passed prohibiting discrimination based on caste, but in reality, the system is in full vitality and still used.

People take this as self-evident because they have been raised with this knowledge. Even schools often tolerate this kind of inequality.

Nobody can run from their heritage; even their family name refers to their caste and everything related to it. Social status doesn't automatically mean material wealth; for example, marriages are usually only made within the castes.

The moment a child is born, they belong to a caste, or status, and all their opportunities are determined by this: education, life partner, profession. People from the lowest caste are discriminated against. They can't possess land, and they can neither drink from public water sources nor touch food at public events. Dalit women are even more downgraded than the men of this caste—they have to accept the dirtiest and despised professions and they are often victims of prostitution. Hierarchy is not just between the castes but also within the castes themselves—for example, in the lowest Dalit caste.

Marriages

Nepali marriages are like family transactions, and most of them are arranged by the parents. Hindus have a belief – marriage is decided in heaven. Parents choose a suitable candidate according to caste, class and education. They also examine the horoscope to determine compatibility, and if everything seems to match, you can set the date. It must be mentioned, though, that among young people, love marriages are becoming more and more popular.

Nepalese wedding. Ceremonial washing of bride's feet before the marriage.

Shutterstock, Lesia Povkh

Same-sex marriages

In 2010, the Nepali Government had a plan to accept a law that permits same-sex marriages. That would have given wealthy Western homosexuals the option to marry in the base camps of Mount Everest (Jomolungma) and to offer other interesting ceremonies to minorities arriving from foreign countries. Generally, Asian countries don't look too kindly on homosexual tourists, but Nepal is a little more liberal and wants to change attitudes, and in doing so, boost the tourist industry, or economy. Until the law changed in 2007, same sex-couples were ostracised, and their relationships were considered a crime that could carry sentences of up to two years of imprisonment. Discussions around same-sex marriages have been going on for many years now, but without any results.

Temple of Pashupatinath

The famous Pashupatinath Temple, which sits on the holy Bagmati river in Kathmandu, is dedicated to the god Shiva's reincarnation, Pashupati. It's a temple complex under UNESCO's protection. Though it is the oldest and biggest Hindu temple in a city that is advertised as a tourist magnet, it leaves non-Hindus behind closed doors.

Why do some sanctuaries stay closed to us? I have heard two answers, but I don't know if they are true: 1. Non-Hindus are not familiar with the temple's etiquette and might not behave appropriately, and 2. Cows are sacred in Nepal, and killing or eating one can be grounds for significant punishment (jail time, fines or both). Since 2015, according to the Nepali constitution, the cow is the national animal of Nepal. Many tourists, though, enjoy delicious meals made of beef, so the Hindus don't wish to pollute their sanctuaries with their presence.

Near the temple, on the banks of the holy Bagmati river, tourists watch the cremation ceremonies of the dead, where ashes are thrown directly into the river. The dead body is carried to the river for a while and washed with holy water, a *tilaka* mark is made on the forehead, and some other spiritual acts are performed. The body, wrapped in linen by family and friends, is then carried to the cremation ghat by the river.

Ceremonies are held by male relatives who have just cut their hair, leaving only a small tuft on the back of their head. *Tonsure*, or cutting the hair, is a deed that symbolizes overcoming pride and eliminating your ego. This deed is a sacrifice to the God, at the same time symbolizing sacrificing one's beauty. Generally, female relatives and acquaintances of the departed watch the ceremony from further away. Not all departed ones are burnt. For example, holy men are buried in the earth's soil. Little children are also not sent to the funeral pyre because their souls don't need to be purged. Suicide victims and murderers are also often not sent to the funeral pyre.

The Bagmati river flows from Kathmandu to the Indian holy river Ganges, where the same rituals are held. There's a guesthouse near *Ghat*, where old or terminally ill people come to die. What more can a Hindu's soul desire than to die in such a sacred place, going straight to the funeral purge from there and becoming part of the river as ash. There are many smaller sanctuaries and lots of holy men, or *sadhus,* in orange robes around the temple. These are the ascetics who have renounced worldly life, pleasures, relatives and friends; they spend their time meditating and living on alms. They live in caves and small cell-like dwellings in the Pashupatinathi area. By living in austerity and doing spiritual practices, *sadhus* hope to burn off a lot of karma and get an even better break in the next life. Their real main goal is to reach *moksha*, or liberation, and not to come back to this cycle of the wheel of life. To be a *sadhu*, you need to find a guru, or spiritual teacher, under whose hand to study and practise and serve. When the time is right, ceremonies are performed to obtain ordinances from the guru or teacher to attain *sadhu* status. There are millions of sadhus in the world, and they mainly live in India. There are holy women who are called *sādhvī* or *sādhvīne*. You can also meet lots of them in Kathmandu near the Bagmati river. The temple of Pashupatinath is mainly inhabited by men devoted to the god Shiva, who cover their bodies with ashes taken from the cremation grids of the dead, believing that this is the ultimate protection against cold, heat and rain. The procedure is also believed to provide protection from all evil. Many *sadhus* around the holy river are very keen to pose for the camera for a small donation. However, in tourist spots such as Pashupatinath, there are also con artists around to extort money from tourists.

When Nepal was still a kingdom, I happened to be in a crowd around Pashupatinath Temple during a festival dedicated to Shiva, Shivratri. It was a true experience. One of the biggest and most important events was full of special-looking holy men and other people. There were attractive holy men in robes: tall, beards almost to their bellybuttons, shaggy rasta hair, huge and smaller *rudraksha* prayer beads on their necks and wrists. Some of them were completely naked, and some were covered only by ashes taken from the funeral pyre. Some read mantras, some communicated with tourists, some were just lying around and some participated in wrestling matches between *sadhus*. There, at the festival dedicated to the god Shiva, apart from the sweet smell of incense and the blue-grey smoke from the burning rituals of the dead, there was also a blue smoky curtain of sadhus' hashish, which was enjoyed to the fullest from the mighty great pipes...

Sadhus, or holy men, posing in the Pashupatinath Temple complex, Kathmandu, Nepal.

Temple of Pashupatinath, Kathmandu, Nepal.

Pashupatinath Temple complex, Kathmandu, Nepal.

Photos by Heli Grauberg, 2019

Writer and doctor Ernst Muldashev in the Nepali Embassy in 1999

A famous Russian doctor and acknowledged writer Ernst Muldashev writes in his book *In Search of the City of God* about a meeting with ambassador Vladimir Vassilyevich (Vassiljevitš) Ivanov and diplomat Shamil Alimhanovitsh Nugayev (Šamil Alimhanovitš Nugajev) in the Nepali Russian Embassy. The topic of securing Chinese visas quickly changed to Nepali life and habits.

The ambassador told Muldashev about his mystical experience in Nepal – there was a glowing circle floating above a stupa. He added, "There are more than enough miracles in Nepal." Vladimir Vassilyevich said: "You can't kill anyone, not even a rat or a fly. One time I saw a rat in my pool and killed it. Almost at the same time my cheek swelled up!" The ambassador shared one more example of how a famous writer (let's not mention names) wrote in his book about this Nepalese custom as a pre-Flood primitiveness. As soon as the book was published, the writer fell through the toilet and almost drowned there in his cottage near Moscow.

Vladimir Vassilyevich added that it's as if only good deeds are permitted in this country, and evil deeds are prohibited in advance. Locals allegedly say that the Nepalese stupas are behind it; they are built according to an ancient plan and they enhance people's good thoughts and destroy evil ones.

Stupa of Boudhanath, Nepal, Kathmandu. Heli Grauberg, 2019

INTERESTING FACTS ABOUT TIBET

Tibet

Tibet is a country on the roof of the world—the closest place to the sky on Earth. It's a country with an average plateau height of 4,500 metres above sea level and 40% less oxygen to breathe than elsewhere. Tibet is a place where tongues are shown as a traditional greeting. It is a land of wonderful monasteries and yak teas, mantras and Buddhist monks—full of ineffable power and spirituality. A land of powerful nature. In Tibet, Buddhism permeates the activities and thoughts of all ordinary people. Entry requires a visa, a special permit and a commitment to be part of a tour group, always accompanied by a local Chinese official tour guide or guard. From time to time, for political and other reasons, various areas of Tibet are closed to foreign tourists for shorter or longer periods.

Tibet, located in Inner Asia, was an independent country from 1913 to 1951 and was annexed in 1950 by the People's Republic of China. The Tibet Autonomous Region covers less than half of historic Tibet; the rest was combined with other provinces during the Chinese occupation. The capital, Lhasa, at 3,650 meters above sea level, is one of the highest cities in the world.

Tibetan history goes back centuries. Tibet was one of the most powerful Asian countries in the 7th century. After the fall of the empire in the 9th century, the land has been split between different powers.

On February 13, 1913, Dalai Lama XIII, Thubten Gyatso, declared Tibet independent and declared that all ties with the Qing dynasty of China, which had fallen from power, were null and void. Until 1950, it was a *de facto* independent state, with everything that went with that status: territory, government, insignia, money, military and legislation. However, the Communists, who won the civil war in 1949, proclaimed the People's Republic of China and automatically considered Tibet part of the People's Republic of China. Tibetan representatives were also forced to sign a treaty recognising the sovereignty of the Tibetan people, which falsely promised to leave Tibetan culture and the political and religious system intact. At first, the young Dalai Lama XIV, Tenzin Gyatso, tried to cooperate with the communist government, but this proved impossible.

Once the Communists were in power, they started to undermine Tibetan everyday life and eradicate Buddhism. In 1959, a Tibetan uprising against Chinese authorities took place. It was bloody, and many people lost their lives. After an unsuccessful uprising, Dalai Lama Tenzin Gyatso was forced to flee to India. He was followed by approximately 100,000 fellow countrymen (by some data it was even half a million). The years between 1959 and 1962 brought Tibet famine, among other things.

The second half of the sixties saw the start of the Cultural Revolution. Statistics show that 6,254 monasteries were closed and destroyed by the Chinese, 1.2 million Tibetans were killed and over 100,000 were sent to concentration camps (these numbers vary from source to source). An alien way of life was imposed on the locals. Mass resettlements of Chinese were organised in Tibetan areas, with the result that the majority population of the former capital, Lhasa, is now Chinese. In the eighties, they suddenly discovered that monasteries were of cultural and historical value, and the shrines were restored. Building processes were controlled by the Communist Party. The 1980s opened the door to foreigners via tourism.

In Spring of 2018 and 2019, approximately 30,000 monks and nuns all over the Tibetan Autonomous Republic were supposed to take exams about the Chinese legislation, which consisted, for example, of legal acts about religion, anti-espionage, the Chinese constitution and other questions important to China. Those who refused to take the exam were supposed to be arrested, interrogated or controlled by other measures. Officials from the ranks of the country's United Workers' Party helped conduct testing procedures in the monasteries. They also gave lessons on how to resist the Dalai Lama, an enemy of the state, and all Tibetan separatism. The conduct of the examinations at Sera, Ganden, Drepung and other monasteries was inspected by senior Chinese officials (*Tibet Watch*, May 2019).

Tibetan family.

*Shutterstock,
Thampitakkull Jakkree*

Potala Palace – former home of XIV Dalai Lama Tenzin Gyatso, Lhasa, Tibet.

*Shutterstock,
Hung Chung Chih*

Dalai Lama Tenzin Gyatso

"My religion is simple. My religion is kindness." *XIV Dalai Lama*

Who is Tenzin Gyatso, XIV Dalai Lama that the big and mighty China fears and hates so much? A dangerous separatist whom China has called a "wolf in monks' robes"? This is a man because of whom well-known car manufacturer Mercedes-Benz had to apologise to China in 2018 for hurting its people's feelings. The sin was that the car company had used the Dalai Lama's quote in an advertisement post on Instagram: "Look at situations from all angles, and you will become more open. Start your week with a fresh perspective on life from the Dalai Lama." Also, many Western artists have been slapped with travel bans to China because of him. Local Tibetans have been arrested and tortured for owning his photograph.

The Dalai Lama is undoubtedly one of the most well-known and popular individuals in the world: Tibetan spiritual leader, Nobel Peace Prize laureate, recipient of honorary doctorates from many of the world's universities, honorary citizen of many countries, recipient of numerous prizes and author of many books.

His Holiness the XIV Dalai Lama Tenzin Gyatso was born on 6 July 1935 into a Tibetan peasant family. At the age of only two, Tenzin underwent a series of trials, which resulted in his being recognised as the successor of the 13th Dalai Lama, and he was awarded the title of Dalai Lama. In Tibetan Buddhism, the Dalai Lama is considered the reincarnation of Avalokiteshvara, the god of compassion (Bodhisatva); a human being who is able to transfer his consciousness to the next birth and is able to control where and when he is born. Once the Dalai Lama has been found, he must receive teaching from the right spiritual teachers. In 1939, Tenzin Gyatso moved to Lhasa and settled with his family in Potala Palace, and at the age of six began his religious studies to become a Buddhist monk. For most of the critical period when China began to encroach on Tibet, the 14th Dalai Lama was only a child and, later, an adolescent, and political decisions were often made on his behalf. In 1959, after the Tibetans' failed uprising against Chinese occupation, Tenzin Gyatso was forced to flee the country and formed a government-in-exile in Dharamsala, India. In 2011, the XIV Dalai Lama voluntarily gave up political power in the government-in-exile, retaining the position of the highest spiritual leader.

The leader elected by the Tibetans in exile (President of Central Tibetan Administration and the political successor to His Holiness the Dalai Lama of Tibet) is now Harvard Law graduate Lobsang Sangay, and secular power is in the hands of the government-in-exile in Dharmsala.

A Nobel Peace Prize laureate since 1989, His Holiness the XIV Dalai Lama Tenzin Gyatso has been declared the greatest enemy of the Chinese. As a result of constant brainwashing, a large part of the Chinese population believes this. For example, possessing a photo of the Dalai Lama can cause very serious problems, and bringing the picture into the country is forbidden. His Holiness has offered the Republic of China a compromise: that Tibet will remain part of the PRC, provided that Tibetans are granted meaningful autonomy. He has tried to find peaceful solutions to the conflicts by renouncing the demand for independence, but all offers of compromise to China have run into the sand. Peaceful protests by the Tibetan people are suppressed by force, followed by repression: imprisonments, shootings and torture.

Chinese-Tibetan politics has completely failed, and persecutions abound: excluding Tibetan language from primary schools, censure, taking over the management of Tibetan monasteries, resettling nomadic pastoralists to barracks, ill-considered extraction of natural resources. However, mineral-rich Tibet is unlikely to be set free by China.

It is not uncommon for Tibetans to set themselves on fire in protest against Chinese rule – in other words, to carry out a non-violent fight for freedom. Since 2009, more than 140 monks have set themselves on fire to attract the world's attention (*The New York Times*, 2016).

On the official website of His Holiness the XIV Dalai Lama Tenzin Gyatso, you can find interesting facts about his life and activities – for example, how the future Dalai Lama recognised items belonging to the previous Dalai Lama XIII. The little boy shouted to the representatives sent by the Tibetan government to search for the new reincarnation, "These are mine!" Also, his mother later recalled an incident upon arrival in Lhasa when the little Dalai Lama announced that his teeth were in a summer residence in Norbulingka. The boy immediately recognised the box found in the house and inside were the dentures belonging to the previous Dalai Lama XIII. Even today, there are many examples from both the East and the West where simple people remember places, relatives, friends and personal belongings from their past lives.

The website also reveals that from the moment the Dalai Lama was born, a pair of crows arrived on the roof of his house, and the birds continued to visit every morning. Exactly the same crow story is recorded in the old chronicles for the four previous Dalai Lamas (Dalai Lamas I, VII, VIII, XII).

China has announced that after the current religious leader has left the earth, it will choose the new Dalai Lama according to the Chinese laws and regulations. However, His Holiness the XIV Dalai Lama has said that when he is around 90, he will consult with senior lamas of Tibetan Buddhism, the public and other followers of Tibetan Buddhism to decide whether to continue with an institution such as the Dalai Lama at all. If they decide to continue the recognition of the XV Dalai Lama's rebirth, His Holiness will leave this task to Dalai Lama Gaden Phodrang Trust, so the whole process will take place according to the old traditions. The current Dalai Lama will also leave clear written instructions for this purpose. Candidates selected for political reasons will certainly not be accepted or recognised. The tradition of the Dalai Lama as a political and religious leader dates back to 1642 in Tibet.

I have made several attempts to meet His Holiness XIV Dalai Lama. In 2007, while attending English language courses in India thanks to a scholarship from the Indian government, my friend Maria, who was also attending the same course, and I took an 11-12-hour night bus. From New Delhi, the night bus took us to the village of McLeod Ganj in Dharmsala, where His Holiness lives and where the office of the government-in-exile is located. At that time, the Dalai Lama was away on a trip, and it was not possible to see him or hear his teachings, but we wandered in the village (by some estimates, a town), full of bald monks and nuns in orange and red robes. A bit Western looking, McLeod Ganj, also called Little Lhasa, is like a little Tibet in the middle of India, with many Tibetan exiles living there. It's full of Buddhists and tourists and volunteers from the West, the latter offer a helping hand in health care, education and other necessities. People also come to McLeod Ganj to receive Buddhist teachings and find inner peace. For the locals, handicrafts and hospitality are the main sources of income.

Tibetan craft markets are full of beautiful jewellery, prayer beads and prayer wheels. There are plenty of restaurants. You get delightful *momos* (dumpling-like food filled with meat or vegetables), Tibetan bread, noodle soup and other tasty things. A small café in the village of McLeod Ganj is where I had the tastiest pancakes in my life.

On this 2007 trip, I was a little nauseous, so I visited the Tibetan exile medical doctor. She measured my pulse and asked me to show her my tongue. In return, I could buy some medicine that looked like sheep dung from the doctor's office. Without having met the Dalai Lama, we had to make the 11–12-

hour bus journey back to New Delhi, India's capital – we were expected to be back in class on Monday morning.

Exactly 10 years later, in 2017, I joined a group in Estonia organised by Roy Strider to travel to Riga, where The XIV Dalai Lama was offering two days of Buddhist teachings. As a student of His Holiness, Roy managed to reach an agreement with the organisers of the Dalai Lama's visit (and who knows who else) beforehand, and negotiated the right to take a group photo of Estonians with the Dalai Lama. So, we gathered in Riga, behind the stage of Skonto Hall, hoping to get a successful photograph. And then came His Holiness… He drove in a big car, accompanied by security guards in dark suits and other characters, right behind Skonto Hall's stage. It was immediately before the second day's teachings. Seeing our anxious Estonian group waiting for a joint picture with Roy, he stepped closer. Wearing a simple robe and a warm smile, he blessed us all. While we were posing for the picture, he happened to take my hand. Those twenty seconds of light hand-holding from the Dalai Lama brought tears of happiness to my eyes. We Estonians had gotten our photo with His Holiness…

Group from Estonia with XIV Dalai Lama Tenzin Gyatso, Riga, Latvia. Roy Strider's private collection, 2017

Panchen Lama

Second in importance to the Dalai Lama in Tibetan Buddhism is the Panchen Lama. The Panchen Lama has a very important role; his role is both political and spiritual. In May 1995, the Chinese abducted the six-year-old Panchen Lama, Gedhun Choekyi Nyima, from his home, and the boy has not been seen or heard from since. China claims that the Panchen Lama is living a normal life and doesn't want to be bothered. Gedhun Choekyi Nyima is the world's youngest political prisoner. The boy was recognised by the XIV Dalai Lama as the reincarnation of the previous high religious leader, the Panchen Lama. Although the Chinese did not acknowledge the Dalai Lama's choice, considering it illegal, they still kidnapped a six-year-old boy with his parents. Despite pleas from Tibetan human rights organisations, the government and many other organisations to know the whereabouts of the Panchen Lama, no information has come from the Chinese so far. Six months after the kidnapping, China announced that it had found a new reincarnation of the Panchen Lama in the form of a Tibetan boy. The new religious leader lives in Beijing, seldomly visits Tibet and is active in the government of the People's Republic of China. As for the Tibetans, they call him a fake Panchen.

Tim Widden, a British expert in age progression and facial reconstruction who helps find missing people, has been asked by the International Tibet Network's (ITN) Political Prisoners Campaign Working Group to examine a childhood photo of Gedhun Choekyi Nyima and create a picture of what the now-30-year-old 11th Panchen Lama might look like today. The image was first revealed on 23 April 2019 on the BBC's *The One Show*.

Buddhism in Tibet

The ancient tradition of Buddhism, or the study of transforming and developing consciousness and liberation from suffering, spread from India to Tibet around the 7th to the 9th century. There are no gods in Buddhism in the usual sense, but there are people who have gained divine powers, and the most famous of them is Buddha Siddhārtha Gautama, who was born in the Nepali village Lumbini. Just after his birth, it was predicted that Siddhārtha would become a monk after seeing the world's suffering. This young son of a nobleman left home, and on his journey, he met sick and old people. He met with ascetics and realised that life is suffering. The young man decided to join a group of five carnal ascetics, and in six years he came to understand that neither of the extreme paths—pleasure nor asceticism—led to true knowledge. The future Buddha decided to continue along the road alone. He sat under a tree, waiting for enlightenment. After a long meditation, this son of a nobleman, Siddhārtha Gautama, became Buddha. He reached nirvana and was freed from the reincarnation circle. Out of his great compassion for humankind, he started to pass on his knowledge during his lifetime. Buddha died when he was 80, consciously breaking the chain of rebirth and ascending to a higher form of being, or nirvana.

Buddha formulated four noble truths: 1. Life is suffering, as are birth, death, aging and illness. 2. The cause of suffering is the will to live—the longing for sensuality and pleasures. 3. Suffering can be ended when the longing for life is gone. 4. There is an eight-part pathway to awakening and to the extinguishing of the will to live (overcoming suffering).

When a person has attained awakening, that higher consciousness offers the possibility of leaving for nirvana for good. Deciding not to take that opportunity reveals a profound compassion for people and the presence of a very noble person, or *bodhisattva*, who chooses the circle of reincarnation, or *samsara*, to help spur other people to honourable deeds with their example. His Holiness the 14th Dalai Lama Tenzin Gyatso, who is currently living in exile in India, is the earthly embodiment of the compassionate Buddha Avalokiteshvara.

Reincarnation. Tibetan Buddhists believe in rebirth, or reincarnation, by which a person's soul will be born into a new body after death. Reincarnation usually happens after a possible pause and judgment day. Depending on the karma of this and previous lives, the person will be born again as a human, animal, god or (why not?) a caterpillar.

Karma, in Sanskrit, means deed. It's a general rule of cause and consequence. It encompasses every mental, verbal or physical act that a person commits every moment, along with its consequences. In other words, you reap what you sow. Some deeds have an immediate result, but some won't be revealed until years later, or maybe even in subsequent lives. Buddhists and Hindus believe that doing good deeds and thinking noble thoughts helps one gather good karma that will have positive consequences in either this life or the next.

Mantras, meditation and mandalas take a central place in Tibetan Buddhists' practices. Mantras are the sounds of the Universe, and every mantra corresponds to a mantra bearer or deity. By saying the mantra, you call the necessary mantra bearer to yourself (like a phone call).

Om Mani Padme Hum is one of the main mantras in Tibet that is associated with the compassion bodhisattva Avalokiteshvara. This mantra is carved into stones or written on the paper placed in the prayer wheel. Such will supposedly enhance the effect of the mantra. Mantras are also mumbled whenever one has the chance; hearing *Om Mani Padme Hum* is rather common during visits to the shops or markets.

There are many forms of meditation in Tibetan Buddhism, but there are two that are perhaps most commonly practised: analytical meditation (meditation based on the study and exploration of Buddhist texts) and concentration meditation (which involves calming the mind through the repetition of mantras, breath observation and other techniques). These meditations are often combined in Tibetan Buddhism.

A *mandala* is a geometrical shape symbolising the samsara of rebirth, or the existential cycle – death, birth, rebirth. Mystical cosmic shapes are used during rituals and as helpers during meditation. In Tibetan Buddhism, coloured sand mandalas are created from texts based on the Buddha's teachings. These are shapes assembled with great precision, mote by mote, by specially trained monks reciting prayers and mantras. When the mandala is finished, after several days of work, it is swept up and thrown into flowing river. It's a symbol of the impermanence of everything.

Ahimsa is the principle of non-violence towards all living things. The killing of anyone is a very ugly act in the Buddhist mind. True Buddhists also spare the life of a fly or other insect by fishing it out of a drinking cup and drying it. Naturally, to save a life.

Before the Chinese annexation and the Cultural Revolution, Tibet was home to many Buddhist monasteries, and Buddhism was predominant for centuries. Despite the efforts of the Chinese authorities, Buddhism has remained intact in the country.

Buddha figure in one of the Burang county Buddhist monastery, Tibet. Heli Grauberg, 2016

Rules for entering Tibet

In order to enter Tibet, a tourist first needs a Chinese visa and a special permit, and it is mandatory to book a Chinese tour guide for the whole duration of the planned trip. If you wish to travel outside Tibet, you will need to apply for permits for the planned areas and arrange private transport outside Lhasa, as public transport is prohibited for tourists outside the capital. All the necessary packages can be booked through local tourist offices. Major changes took place in 2008 when the PRC changed the rules for foreigners travelling to Tibet to make it more inconvenient.

Bringing the Dalai Lama's pictures, books and recordings of speeches to Tibet is prohibited, and owning a Tibetan flag or picture of the flag is illegal. One also has to be careful when taking the *Lonely Planet* travel guide, because those books have been confiscated from tourists by Chinese officials (*Lonely Planet*).

Tibet is usually closed to foreigners in February and March, and often at other unexpected times, too. A very sensitive day, 10 March, falls within this period - Tibetan National Uprising Day. On the anniversary of this bloody uprising in 1959, Tibet is closed to foreigners every year, just in case, to prevent protests and disturbances. This season also includes the celebration of the Tibetan New Year *Losar*.

Journalists and diplomats are not allowed to arrange their own travel to Tibet through a travel agency; they can only do so with an invitation from the government of the People's Republic of China (*The Diplomat*, 2019).

After a long eight-year wait, Norwegians can finally re-enter Tibet as of April 2018. The awarding of the Norwegian Nobel Peace Prize to human rights activist Liu Xiaobo angered Greater China, leading to a ban on Norwegian entry into Tibet.

Flag of China, Tibet. Heli Grauberg, 2019

Etiquette and taboos

Tibet travel agency websites highlight local etiquette and a few taboos that travellers to the far-off land should know a little about.

You eat and drink in quiet and usually use only your right hand for eating. Tibetan families offer food until the pot is empty, and a polite way to refuse food is to put your hands together as if in prayer and ask for forgiveness. For religious reasons, fish is not eaten in many Tibetan regions, as the fish is one of the eight sacred symbols in Tibetan Buddhism. While visiting, only the hostess serves drinks; self-service is out of the question. A polite guest never drinks his mug completely empty, but leaves a little at the bottom, because a drop at the bottom of the cup symbolises continued abundance. If the cup is empty, you can be sure that the hosts will keep serving the tea or wine until the guest realises what is going on. You always have to hold the cup with two hands – this symbolises respect.

When visiting someone, you should take a small gift with you; traditionally, in addition to other small souvenirs, it should also include butter tea and beer. You give the gift with two hands and a slight bow. Local tradition is to give a part of the gift back – this should not be interpreted as an insult.

It's also inappropriate to point your feet towards people when you're sitting, and touching children's heads is taboo in this country.

Take off your hat when entering a temple, and make sure your clothing covers your calves – it's very disrespectful to enter the sanctuary in shorts or a miniskirt. You should speak quietly in the temple and not touch anything, because many pieces are very sacred. Taking photographs is usually prohibited, but some temples allow it for a small fee. Sitting on the ground facing the altar and other holy objects, stretching your legs out and walking in front of a person who is praying are all regarded as disrespectful and should be avoided. You should move clockwise in or around the sanctuary (except in Bön temples).

You should definitely not step over food or any sacred objects such as prayer flags. Some mountain regions are filled with colourful Buddhist prayer flags; walk around them or, if possible, raise them up and pass under them.

If you wish to take a photo of a Tibetan, you must ask permission, because many locals believe that when they are photographed, they will be stuck in the photo even after death and won't be able to move on. Those who do allow you to take pictures will most likely expect a small donation or gift.

You should not panic if a local shows you their tongue. This is a traditional greeting with a long history. Showing their tongue is a symbolic act; they are letting you know that they are not a demon and don't have evil intentions toward you.

When travelling with your partner, it is advisable not to show affection in public, as this is also taboo.

In Tibet, it's good to have little gifts for local children at hand. They get excited about things like pencils, felt-tip pens, candies, notebooks and other similar trinkets.

Child in Tibet.
Heli Grauberg, 2019

Tibetan kitchen

Tibetan cuisine is based on yak and goat meat, barley flour, dairy products and noodles.
The traditional breakfast of Tibetans is *tsampa* and yak butter tea. *Tsampa* dough is made of roasted barley flour to which is added butter tea; the dough is then formed into ball-shaped loaves. They are eaten with every meal, and *tsampa* is great to take on the road. Like bread.

Butter tea, or *po cha,* is a traditional beverage in Tibet and in Tibetan communities in Nepal and India. It symbolizes local life and national culture. This beverage has a high calorie count and a warming effect, so it's beneficial to drink in the highland conditions. Moisturizing your lips with butter tea also prevents your lips from cracking in windy Tibet. Butter tea is like coffee for a Western person – it's part of the daily routine. They say that Tibetans drink up to 40 small cups of tea in a day that are made of black tea, yak butter, water, salt and cream or milk.

Here is one of many authentic recipes:

2–3 teaspoons of tea, 2 teaspoons of Himalayan salt, 2/3 cup of light cream, 2 teaspoons of yak milk butter.

Boil 2 cups of water, then add *pu-erh* tea (Chinese dark tea) to the boiling water, heat at a low temperature 3-5 minutes and then boil the mixture for a long time. Add salt and cream and mix, heating it at a low temperature. Finally, put in the butter and whip the tea until it's foamy. Traditionally, the tea is whisked in a tube-like utensil called a *chandong*. When the tea is ready, it's poured into a thermos and drunk throughout the day.

Although the tea is called yak butter tea, a yak is actually a male animal. The female is called a *dri,* so the tea could be called dri butter tea.

Momos are what we might call little dumplings. Momo dough is made of flour and water (you can also add soda). Momos are filled with meat or different vegetables. They are either steamed or fried, according to preference.

Tibetans really love sausages – blood sausages and white or grit sausages are very popular. Another popular thing is homemade barley beer, which is kindly offered to guests.

In 1988, the Chinese built a beer factory in Lhasa that is the highest brewery in the world. *Lhasa* beer is made in the European style, but the water for the beer comes straight from Himalaya and the barley from the local Tibetan fields.

Few crops can be grown on the rooftop of the world, so Tibetan cuisine is a bit sparse for us.

In Tibet, as in many other Asian countries, there is an unwritten rule for tourists: "Boil it, cook it, peel it or forget it!" Bananas are easy, but an apple, for example, should be peeled. Often, salads may not have been washed with boiled water, and yoghurt may also contain uncooked water. For the Western stomach, uncooked and undercooked food can have really unfortunate consequences. In Tibet, as in India and the Arab world, people often eat with their bare hands, using only their right hand. The left hand is considered unclean in these cultures because it is used in the toilet. It is not even appropriate to receive food with the left hand.

Yaks

Who are these marvellous animals with mighty long horns, a height of two metres and a coat that almost reaches the ground? These are powerful Tibetan yaks, adapted to the highlands, with big lungs and heart. The yak has three times more blood cells than a normal bovine, allowing this large animal to live on the roof of the world. A thick, dense coat helps this member of the cattle family to survive winter temperatures of up to minus 30 degrees – when it snows, the thick coat acts like a blanket to protect its sides. Yaks are good at traversing steep slopes and very difficult roads, but they can also cross swamps and shallow riverbeds. They can walk up to 15 kilometres a day, carrying 100-200 kilograms on their backs. They start carrying heavy loads at around two years of age and often live for more than 20 years. Yaks are mainly black or brown, but there are also grey and even white ones.

Yaks are crucial for those locals who live in difficult conditions because they are one of the few animals in Tibet whose body parts are almost all used.

Yaks provide milk, cheese, butter, yoghurt, butter tea and high-protein, almost fat-free meat. In summertime, yak meat is dried. It is even eaten raw in the wintertime. Their blood is used to make blood sausages, and bones find their way into the craftsmen's hands. Yak butter is used to make candles and sculptures. Yaks' outer wool is woven into tent fabric and braided into cords, and the felted *charas* used in religious ceremonies are made of soft underwool. Tail hair finds its way into wigs and fake moustaches used in the opera. Skin is used for making boats and aprons, boots and tents. Yaks' heads are considered a symbol of strength and protection; tails symbolize wealth and luck.

These animals don't like to eat grain feed or much of anything else except grass, and if there's not plenty of that, they rather starve. This makes it difficult to use yaks for carrying loads on longer expeditions.

Walking between villages in Tibet, you can see piles of yak dung being dried around the dwellings. Yak dung also helps to heat homes, and yak butter lamps bring light to homes.

Yaks have been so important to Tibetan families that they are called by children's names. Life there has been centred around yaks for the last 2000 years.

Yaks are kind and patient animals. Shutterstock, Arijeet Bannerjee

Yaks carrying loads around Mount Kailash, Tibet. Heli Grauberg, 2016

The eagle, a holy bird

These majestic birds with mighty heads and beaks, who fly around the Himalayan skies kilometres up high, are the Tibetan holy eagles. They fly the highest, which is what makes them the creatures that are closest to the gods. They are revered and loved throughout the Himalayas for the very fact that they eat the corpses and carrion that would otherwise pollute the bodies of water used by Tibetans for drinking water. With their large, strong beaks and claws, these winged creatures feed on the corpses of birds and animals. They will not turn their noses up at live animals, either. They adore the bones, from which they get the precious marrow. They have gotten used to taking food from burial grounds for generations, and do a great deal of cleaning after a Sky burial (see the section on the Sky burial).

The bird's body height is about 94-125 cm. They usually live far away from populated areas, near the high rocks. Himalayan eagles love to make a nest in the same place every year; a mating pair stays together and both mother and father bird take care of the chicks.

Landing Himalayan eagle.
Shutterstock, Mousam Ray

Tibetan mastiff

A Tibetan's best friend is a Tibetan mastiff! This loyal breed – a natural watchdog – can be found in Tibet and all over the world. These thick-coated guard dogs have evolved over millennia as a result of harsh living conditions and natural selection. *Drog-Khyi* in Tibetan means nomad dog and also "dog that can be tied up."

Tibetan mastiffs have been herding cattle for thousands of years in Tibet, as well as in Mongolia, Nepal and China – protecting herds and owners from predators such as wolves, bears, leopards and tigers. The small and wrinkled-faced Tibetan mastiff is called *Tsang-Khyi*, which means dog from Tsang or monastery dog. The larger pups of the same litter go to monasteries and temples to work, and the better-built ones are more suited to more active work as herding dogs. Mastiffs are resilient and rugged animals that live in highland conditions on the dry and dangerous Tibetan plateau. They are dominant by nature, so owners are encouraged to show who is in charge of the herd. An adult dog can weigh between 45 and 70 kilograms and coat colours vary quite widely.

There are many legends about the mighty Tibetan mastiff. It's believed that this breed is a reincarnation of people who were just one step away from true awakening and came back as dogs to protect Tibetan people and animals. They believe that the spots above the mastiff's eyes are actually another set of eyes that keep watch even when the dog is sleeping. When danger is near, these animals keep away all malicious people, animals and spirits. A black spot on the chest is a sign of bravery, and a completely white dog brings luck.

Initially, this breed of dog was allowed to be gifted or given away in Tibet, but could not be sold. Lately, Tibetan mastiffs have been valued as one of the most expensive dog breeds, and pups are sold for a million dollars in China. In 2014, a Chinese property developer bought a Tibetan mastiff at a "luxury pet" fair for almost 2 million US dollars (*The Washington Post*, 2014). It is the only country where dogs are sold and bought at such a high price. In Europe, prices range between €1,000 and €5,000, depending on pedigree.

In their homeland, Tibet, they wear a large strong collar called *kekhor* that's made of yak's wool felt and usually coloured red.

The purpose of the collar is to protect the dog from wolves when they must fight to protect the herd. The collar also makes the dog look bigger and can keep away quite a few predators.

There are many Tibetan mastiffs wandering around Mount Kailash with and without their owners. Thankfully, all the dogs wandering around alone are friendly and quite happy to pose for photos.

Tibetan mastiff. In their native Tibet, they wear a sturdy, large-necked kekhor, made from yak wool and usually dyed red.

Shutterstock, Anna Tronova

Rural marriage – polyandry (having several husbands)

The principle of polyandry is simple: all brothers (Tibetan families are often rather big) share the same wife. Polyandry is now banned in China under the Family Law, but it is still quite common in rural Tibet. Such marriages are an economic arrangement, where land is not divided between brothers and labour and household responsibilities are equitably divided. Traditionally, the marriage is arranged beforehand by the parents, and the woman moves into the home of the husband(s).

Usually, the older brother is the one to participate in the wedding ceremony, but sometimes all adult brothers participate. When younger brothers are old enough, they will also join in sharing the wife. The oldest brother is dominant; he has privileges with regard to the wife and assumes the leading role in the household. At the same time, all the brothers share equally in household chores and sexual activities.

This kind of wife-sharing in everyday life and in bed does not seem scandalous or unusual at all for Tibetans. It is customary for a woman to treat all brothers equally and to treat all offspring equally, even if the child's biological father is known. It's always the oldest brother who is called father; younger ones are called uncles.

(For more information, you can look at, for example, Indian Himalayan polyandry, Youtube: Multiple Husbands, *National Geographic*).

The principle of polyandry is simple – all brothers share the same wife.
Shutterstock, Phaendin

Sky burial

Magnificent wide-winged vultures on the alert, waiting for their treat – human flesh. This is the final scene of a Tibetan Sky burial.

The sky burial is a mystical act that a typical tourist's eyes won't see (there are exceptions, of course). My guide was delicately hinting at a mountain around the Kailash area, where those funerals are held.

Sky burials are practised mostly in Tibet, but sometimes in China and Mongolia as well. Three popular places for it are Drigung and Ganden monasteries in Tibet and funeral locations around Larung Gar Buddhist Institute.

Prior to the funeral, the deceased is placed in a sitting position at home and relatives are forbidden from touching him for three days. At this time, the lama, or monks, will say prayers aloud to help the soul pass smoothly into the next life.

When the prayers are done, they crack the spine of the deceased and the body is twisted together and wrapped in a white sheet, so the journey to the heaven funeral location can begin (sometimes they are delivered lying down). In some regions, relatives will stay at home to pray; in some they join the ceremony. Corpse choppers by profession, or *ropyagas,* start by burning juniper and other vegetation that produces aromas that attract vultures. The deceased person's face is placed against a rock, where the *ropyagas* remove their hair and chop the person according to a certain ceremony. Finally, they remove the internal organs.

By that time, the vultures, with their vast two-metre wingspans, will be already waiting to take the deceased to heaven. After fifteen minutes the corpse is gone. Tibetans believe that the eagles are like angels who take the deceased up so they can wait for their rebirth. The body is just a vessel for the soul, and when the soul is gone, it's good to recycle the useless body. Leftover bones from vultures are cracked, and the remains will go to crows and hawks. The last good deed of the deceased in this world is to give everything back to nature.

That's how other beings are saved, too. According to the Buddhist explanation, the eagle will be filled by the human flesh and, thanks to that, will have mercy on some other living being – some animal or bird.

Tibetans are not afraid of dying because for them, it's just a transition to another stage; death is not the end, as it's often considered in other places. As the soul leaves the body, it has no more emotional ties with the body.

It's considered a bad omen when eagles refuse the human flesh. Too dirty to eat! There is a belief that maybe the relatives have not done the necessary rites, or the person did something incredibly evil during their lifetime. This can actually happen if the body is cleaned with disinfectant, because the eagles hate this taste. In this case, the meal is left for the wild dogs you can see wandering around the Tibetan plateau.

It is not a good practice to leave anything of the human body behind, but it has long been known that leftover bones are sometimes used to make ritual musical instruments, teacups, Tibetan music boxes and other sacred objects.

Land is often frozen in Tibet; that makes it hard to dig a grave. A deficit of wood makes cremation impossible also. Sky burial is not just practical, but also a spiritual act.
(See the topic further on Youtube under the keyword: *Sky burial Tibet*.)

Sky burial. Tibetans believe that eagles are like angels who take the dead up to await their new birth.

Shutterstock, Dustin Kerschtien

कैलास

PILGRIMAGE TO MOUNT KAILASH 2016

10th of June – 4th of July

TRANSPORT **ACCOMODATION**
planes   hotels
helicopter   hostels
buses   guesthouses

LONDON
United Kingdom

KATHMANDU
Nepal

NEPALGUNJ
Nepal

SIMIKOT
Nepal

HILSA
Nepal

PURANG
Tibet

DARCHEN
Tibet

DIRAPUK
Tibet

ZUTULPUK
Tibet

DARCHEN
Tibet

LAKE MANASAROVAR
Tibet

The trip begins in the capital of Nepal – Kathmandu. Visiting Boudhanath

KATHMANDU (Nepal)

It was June of 2016 when I arrived in Nepal's capital, Kathmandu, for the third time. At the airport, the colleague of the owner of a local travel company, Krishna, was waiting for me with a big sign saying "HELI". A Nepalese driver drove us in his worn-out car to a hotel located in the city centre, Thamel, where I met Krishna himself soon enough. We sat in the hotel's restaurant and learned that the pilgrimage group that I was supposed to be a part of was already moving towards Mount Kailash, so my departure was not yet certain. Krishna told me I should be ready to start at any time and shouldn't turn off my phone.

My initial plan was to do some volunteering in the Nepal Kathmandu KAT (Kathmandu Animal Treatment) Centre. I had been following the Centre's selfless activities on social media for quite some time. I contacted KAT beforehand and was advised to get vaccinated against rabies. As I only had 1-3 days free from travelling to volunteer, I decided not to get the vaccine (a series of injections in several doses at different times), and so I unfortunately had to give up my job with homeless dogs.

This non-profit organization, KAT, was founded in 2004 by English artist Jan Salter and concentrates on controlling the street dog population, fighting rabies and treating and placing homeless dogs, but also on specific educational programs and other issues concerning animals. In 2004, an agreement was reached with the Kathmandu city government to stop poisoning homeless dogs in the areas where Jan Salter's team worked, and over time, the local authorities have stopped the inhumane slaughter of animals on the streets. Jan Salter, who has since left us, was awarded the MBE by Queen Elizabeth II of England in 2013 for his work with animals in Nepal.

I spent several days in a state of uncertainty, waiting for Krishna's notice. In my heart, I desperately wanted to finally begin my journey to Nepalgunji, to begin my pilgrimage. The long-awaited notification came soon – just three days of sitting around in Kathmandu and it was time to move forward. To be honest, I did not do that much sitting; on the very first day, I called a taxi from the hotel and headed to Boudhanath stupa.

The Boudhanath Stupa is a large stupa with four pairs of hypnotic Buddhist eyes. One of the most important sanctuaries in Kathmandu, it symbolises the whole universe and enlightenment.

The grand building is surrounded by temples, shops and diners. In April 2015, Nepal was hit by an earthquake and the country's largest stupa was damaged. In the summer of 2016, this 14th-century beauty stood miserably broken, surrounded by scaffolding for restoration work and local builders doing their best. By the time this book was published, the stupa had long since been fully restored (completed in November 2016), thanks to a donation of more than 2 million dollars from Buddhist groups and volunteers worldwide and 31 kilos of gold spent on the restoration. A three-day ceremonial cleansing was also carried out, which included dropping flowers from a helicopter onto the stupa.

Around the base of the 36-metre-high giant stupa, 147 niches have been carved into the stone, housing prayer wheels behind which one finds 108 small Buddha figures. From the top of the shrine, prayer flags are suspended from strings, which are believed to send sacred prayers on their way as they flutter in the wind. Movement around a stupa is clockwise and the prayer wheels in rows are to be spun the same way. Hundreds upon hundreds of believers and tourists circle the stupa every day, chanting mantras, twirling prayer wheels and rolling prayer beads between their fingers. On the wheels is the inscription *Om Mani Padme Hum*, and inside the cylinders (you can't see inside, but that's how it's supposed to be) are sacred syllables written on paper, which are activated when spun clockwise. This has the same, and perhaps an even more powerful, effect than simply reciting the mantras.

I started spinning those cylindrical metal wheels too, making a lot of circles around the stupa. All in an effort to purge negativity, remove obstacles, get rid of bad karma and do good for the world with this deed.

After visiting Boudhanath, I headed to Durbar Square in Kathmandu, which was once a truly beautiful part of the city, with its royal palace and temples dedicated to various Hindu gods. Now, due to the 2015 earthquake, it is in a pretty disastrous state. It was so sad to see these collapsed historic buildings resembling large piles of rubbish, that I didn't go to the UNESCO World Heritage site this time.

I did a little shopping and went to rest in the hotel early in the evening. In preparation for the next day, I decided to take a look at my finances. I thought I had left my big red wallet with cash in a locked suitcase while visiting Boudhanath and Durbar Square. When I opened my suitcase in my hotel room, I realized that those three hundred dollars that were meant for expenses during the Tibetan pilgrimage were gone from my wallet. I started to blame myself for being negligent. I was certain I had sleepily pulled out the rolled banknotes on arrival at Kathmandu airport and lost them. Maybe I didn't lose them myself? Maybe somebody secretly came to my hotel room and opened my locked suitcase while

I was out visiting tourist attractions for the whole day? I went to sleep rather grumpy and was in no better state when I woke up. In the morning, I made a decision to not think about this incident and went to a salon in Thamel to rejuvenate myself. Here, a young Nepali woman in a hotel spa gave really interesting complex massages for a great price. For some time, she sat on my spine and twisted and oiled my body parts, combining classical massage, Japanese puncture massage, Thai therapy and who knows what else. After this refreshing experience, my bad mood was wiped away. Compared to Europe, massage is cheap in Nepal and there are plenty of salons in Kathmandu. Restorative massages are especially popular among mountaineers after the hikes.

Two and a half years later, I found the 300 dollars in the inner pocket of the small purse that had been with me in Nepal and on other trips. When did I put them there? I guess after buying a Nepali visa on the border, being completely sleep-deprived and landing at my hotel exhausted from the trip. I was not happy about finding the money at all; I was embarrassed, because I had considered the possibility that somebody had touched my suitcase in my hotel room.

Boudhanath stupa. Kathmandu, Nepal. Restoration works after the earthquake.

Next to Boudhanath stupa, Kathmandu, Nepal.

3x Heli Grauberg, 2016

Bird's eye view of Boudhanath stupa and Kathmandu. Maksim Semin, Shutterstock

First internal flight – Nepalgunj

NEPALGUNJ (Nepal)

Boy, was I happy when Krishna announced on Wednesday that I could move on from Kathmandu. He had an idea of which flights and pilgrimage groups to put me in before heading to the mountain. I packed my backpack with all the necessary things and left my big suitcase in the hotel's luggage room.

The first internal flight took me to the city of Nepalgunj, south of Kathmandu. It's one of the hottest places in Nepal; in summertime, the temperature can reach over 40 degrees. It really was extremely hot. The hotel had very nice accommodations, with an outdoor pool and a big garden where one could relax before the big adventure. It was a delight to enjoy a tasty Nepali and Indian dinner in the verdant yard. By then, it was already dark, but some men staying at the hotel were still enjoying the pool. I did not see any of the female guests swimming, so I passed on the chance. In the evening, I messaged some of my friends on the Internet and had a warm shower. This was the last luxury of this trip, because my later accommodations would be more modest (Purang Hotel in the middle of my trip was rather okay, though).

Acclimatising at the home of a Nepalese family in Simikot

SIMIKOT (Nepal)

The next internal flight departed early the next morning for Simikot, in the Humla district of Nepal. Krishna had written the name of a man on a slip of paper; I was to find this man in a local guesthouse and he would help me from there. I found this small, middle-aged Nepali man and he led me to the guesthouse, where I had to share a tiny room with five mature, middle-aged Indian women. They were also pilgrims, and they had already taken over the cramped room – some lying on a mattress on the floor, some resting on a comfy bed. Fortunately, I manged to avoid having to navigate this situation;

for an extra fee, I used the home-stay service of a friendly mother who was raising two lovely boys and shared the house with her immediate family.

I met large groups of Indian pilgrims in front of the Simikot diner who approached me unexpectedly, asked questions, took pictures and shoved a big video camera in my face. They even asked me for an interview.

Then, suddenly, the Indian pilgrims started dancing, and I was the one who was filming and photographing them because they had asked me to. Finally, lunch was ready, and I was invited to the diner by complete strangers. I was a little confused, and in that hall filled with spicy aromas, I started on my lunch in solitude. When my lunch time was over, all the big groups were allowed to eat, one at a time. They shouldn't have done it that way. Who came up with such an idea?

Later on in my journey, I met people on the pilgrimage stops who didn't quite understand what a Western person was doing on this trip, and lots of pictures were taken of me as mementos.

On my journey, I made an Indian friend, Amrita, whom I kept meeting again at the pilgrimage stops and doing the *kora* around Mount Kailash.

I was acclimatising in Simikot for two days and nights. I spent the days walking around the village and reading about Mount Kailash in my room. I bought the book I was reading from a bookstore in Thamel in Kathmandu. In the evenings, I ate local bread with the family in the dimly lit kitchen in front of a live fire, drank tea and enjoyed conversing using sign language. Even then, the date of my departure for my next destination, Hilsa, was completely unclear. Early one morning, the hostess knocked on my door, told me something in Nepali and used gestures to let me know I should move on, and quickly. I hurriedly packed my stuff and ran to the small Simikot airport with the hostess, running over dusty hills. I guess Krishna knew exactly where I was staying and had alerted the hostess about the helicopter landing.

Simikot, Nepal. Heli Grauberg, 2016

Indian friend found on the road, Amrita. Hands in prayer and Mount Kailash in the background.

Professor, Ultra Cyclist, Marathoner, wife & loving mother.
Photo from Amrita's private collection, 2016.

Amrita Ranjan 1.05.81-16.11.21. R.I.P.

Helicopter flight to a Nepal-China border village, Hilsa

HILSA (Nepal)

Now the journey to the Nepal-China border village of Hilsa could begin – the very first helicopter flight of my life, among the scenic Nepalese mountains. The helicopter was stuffed to the ceiling with pilgrims' bags, and with great difficulty they squeezed me and an elderly Indian gentleman in. On the sixth day of the trip, I finally met my actual guide, with whom I waited a long day in Hilsa to cross the Nepal-China border. Our main activities in this extremely tiny village were eating, drinking tea and water, and just sitting around in the kitchen, which had been adapted for pilgrims. You have to drink a lot to prevent mountain sickness, which I did out of dread, so I kept having to flush the toilet. The guide was a Nepali man, pleasant but not very chatty, so I spent long hours in the semi-dark kitchen with a book on Mount Kailash I had bought in Kathmandu. Occasionally I would go outdoors to stretch my legs, and as there were a lot of sad looking donkeys wandering around the village, I would pet them as a pastime. In Hilsa, on the Nepal-China border, there were probably as many hardy donkeys as there were locals.

Neither the guide not I had any clue when we would be able to move on again, and we had to entertain ourselves somehow. I managed to meet two Indian men there who spoke English with each other and seemed too well-dressed – in light colours, no less – for this kind of hike. I learned that they had trained for a long time for this pilgrimage and were hoping for the best from this trip.

At the Nepal-China border crossing at the Karnali River bridge, it turned out that my guide had a Chinese visa, but the permit to enter the Kailash region had not yet reached the border. I was confused...Would I be travelling with a group of strangers all alone? With whom? Was I to march on, alone, from there? The guide made a quick call to Krishna, and when he left, he handed me over to a group of Indian pilgrims. I was going to have to join some group on the Chinese side anyway, as they don't let lone trekkers into the Kailash region anymore. So, I had to watch sadly as my guide returned to the Karnali River bridge, back to Nepal. After passing through the Chinese army checkpoint, I drove with the new group to the immigration office. It later turned out that I was to continue my journey with a group of 50-60 Indian pilgrims. What really happened during this moment by the bridge was that I was united with a smallish Indian group that consisted of friends who knew each other well and who take this trip almost every year. I was very happy to meet this small and rather humble group.

The helicopter was packed to the ceiling with pilgrims' bags, and with great difficulty, they squeezed me and an elderly Indian gentleman in.
The journey to Hilsa, Nepal.

Bridge on the border of Nepal-China, River Karnali, Hilsa, Nepal.

In Hilsa, on the Nepal-China border, there were probably as many hardy donkeys as there were locals.

Hilsa, Nepal.

Photos by Heli Grauberg, 2016

Acclimatising in Purang
Visiting the Gongphur cave monastery

PURANG (Tibet)

The journey to Purang (sometimes spelled Burang) began, and from then on, we always had a Chinese tour guide, or "guard", on the bus. Purang is the administrative centre of Purang County in the Tibetan Autonomous Region and has been a popular trading post for centuries for traders from India and Nepal. The town, at 4,755 metres above sea level, has a population of over 9,000 people, according to Wikipedia.

At the hotel where we were staying, during dinner in the restaurant, I was suddenly approached by a Nepali man and told that he was my new guide – Krishna had been working in Kathmandu again. One of his guides, named Umesh, was on his way back to Kathmandu from Kailash with his group and was stopping in Purang, and Krishna's phone call prompted him to rejoin me on the Kailash trek. For Umesh, it was the 46th time he had made a circle around the holy mountain, and by the end of the 2016 pilgrimage season, he would have completed at least 50 circles. I wonder if completing 108 koras gives only pilgrims the opportunity to ascend to nirvana from the chain of reincarnation, or do the kilometres completed on the job also count?

During the same dinner, a woman from Indore, India, came to talk to me. Her name was Sunita, and she was a doctor by profession. She was on her way back home from a pilgrimage and gave me some of her herbs, vitamins, and natural products that I might need. I was really touched.

We were only supposed to spend one night in Purang, but the Chinese told us that too many people had recently died of high-altitude sickness, and we would have to spend an extra night acclimatising. On a brisk run up the stairs to the hotel room, I discovered that it wasn't so easy anymore; I was out of breath. Suddenly, my journey had taken me to 4,755 metres above sea level.

On the first morning, Umesh took me to Gongphur Cave Monastery, just outside the town of Purang. As the monastery is located on a very high hill, the visit was to help me acclimatise. Gongphur is one of the few monasteries in Tibet to have preserved precious sacred artefacts untouched by the Chinese Cultural Revolution. The sanctuary is surrounded by a mystical aura. Five monks currently reside there. Two of us were even allowed to enter a couple of monastery rooms. It was in this special place that I prayed for my pilgrimage to succeed.

Gongphur Monastery is located on the side of the Tegla Kar hill and is open seven days a week. The monastery has a total of six cave temples: the Du-Kang (main hall), where sacred objects are kept on the altar and where monks gather to perform Buddhist practices; the Kagyur Lhakang (Sutra Temple), where 108 books of the teachings of Buddha Shakyamuni are kept; the Gon Khang (Dharma Protector Hall), where the masks and images of Dharma (Buddhist teachings) protectors are displayed; the Palde Lhakang and the Kayab. The latter two are retreat caves used for religious practices in seclusion.

During the Cultural Revolution of the 1960s, many valuable artefacts were lost from the monastery and the caves, staircases and balconies of the sanctuary were demolished. The Red Guards destroyed everything that was old and traditional. Despite this, the monks of the Drikung Kagyu Order and the local people, working together, managed to make a hole in the wall of the main temple, from which sacred objects could be secretly removed at night and deposited in a monastery in Nepal. Nineteen years later, when the Chinese gave Tibetans "religious freedom", monasteries were gradually restored and Gongphur was given a new mantle, with precious Buddhist artefacts finding their way back home (information about the temple: *Kailashzone Charitable Foundation*).

Purang was a place where I was supposed to start taking the medicine packed by Krishna, Diamox, to prevent mountain sickness. The main symptoms of the sickness are headache, nausea, vomiting, tiredness and sleeplessness. I swallowed half a tablet every evening. The side effects were a buzzing in my hands every morning and an extremely frequent need to visit the toilet. Another remedy against mountain sickness is to drink plenty of water, a duty that all pilgrims took seriously.

Young and old alike gather every evening in the central square of Purang to participate in choreographed dancing in front of communist monuments and red flags. One half of the square is occupied by disco lovers, who dance to popular music coming from the speaker to the accompaniment of collective movements. On the other side of the square, a circle is formed; the national dance is a bit like line dancing. This may be one of the only social events or amusements for both young and old in this city.

There were plenty of "No cameras" signs on the streets, and Facebook didn't work the whole time we were in China, because it's banned there.

It was very relaxing to wander around the shops in the historic shopping centre, as I couldn't understand any of the vendors, and if I had asked for anything, they wouldn't have been able to understand English anyway. The electricity was usually off, and you could barely see the goods on the dimly lit shelves.

Purang was the last stop before Mount Kailash where we could take a real shower. All the nights afterward, we slept in the same travel clothes, because the air was cold and the cleanliness of the sheets was questionable, at best (if there were sheets at all). Occasionally, there were open-air toilets, but usually, the only toilet was the beautiful Tibetan countryside.

On my way to Gongphur cave monastery, Tibet.

Photos by Heli Grauberg, 2016

On the way to Gongphur Cave Monastery, Tibet (the monastery can be seen from the hillside). As the monastery is located at a very high altitude, the visit was also supposed to help me acclimatise.

Gongphur is one of the few monasteries in Tibet to have preserved precious sacred artefacts untouched by the Chinese Cultural Revolution.

Local children enjoying our Kailash group taking pictures with Khorzhak Monastery in the backround, Purang, Tibet.

Roommates Bharathi and Chitra, Purang, Tibet.

The pilgrimage begins in Darchen

DARCHEN (Tibet)

The small dusty village of Darchen is located in Purang County, Tibet Autonomous Region, at an altitude of about 4,575 metres above sea level.

Everyone starts their three-day pilgrimage, or *kora* (also known as *parikrama*), from Darchen on the southern slopes of Mount Kailash. Every year, thousands of pilgrims, photographers and hikers arrive to turn this tiny place into an international hub during the peak pilgrimage season. More than 100,000 visitors a year mean that more and more accommodations and diners have to be built.

Darchen is also home to the Tibetan Institute of Medicine and Astrology, founded in 1995 by the Ngari Korsum Association of Tibet in Switzerland. The whole complex has expanded over time and now includes a hospital, a Tibetan medical school with a large library, a Tibetan pharmaceutical department and a guesthouse called Sun and Moon. The medical boarding school, which can house up to 50 students, gives priority to young people aged 15 to 20 from poorer families in the Ngari region (western Tibet). Most of the graduates return to their home communities, but some also find work at Darchen Hospital, and some go on to study at the country's major universities.

The hospital, which is located at the same place as the Institute, mostly uses Tibetan medicine (however, antibiotics are also prescribed for certain illnesses), and most of the plants used in the pharmaceutical industry are harvested from the groves and slopes of the nearby Mount Kailash.

The Tibetan Institute of Medicine and Astrology is intimately involved in various projects to promote health and protect the environment: hygiene efforts, the campaign to keep the area around Mount Kailash clean, promoting environmental education, etc.

Settlements in the Mount Kailash region are expanding, modern technology is being introduced and the lifestyle is radically different from what it was in the 1980s, when the first foreigners were allowed on pilgrimages. Until then, the area had been the exclusive domain of local nomads. One of the aims of the Tibetan Institute of Medicine and Astrology is to instil in students an appreciation of environmental stewardship, so that future doctors can in turn pass on these attitudes to their fellow villagers.

In 2011, the highest institution in Western Tibet suddenly suspended all aid from the Swiss Tibetan Ngari Korsum Association and placed all of the Tibetan Medical and Astrological Institute and its complex under China's own foundation. A pledge was also made to keep the future activities and plans of the Centre in line with the original vision of the Swiss side. Let's hope that the Chinese will keep their promises (*Kailash Projekte*).

We arrived in Darchen in the evening, and for the first time we had an amazing close-up view of the beautiful Mount Kailash, also called the Snow Jewel. The village was lined with small shops where you could bargain quite effectively with the local merchants. I had bought a few souvenirs at a discount from the shop, and had just sat down at the shop door for a moment when the hostess suddenly invited me back inside. I was sure she was trying to pin something on me. When I got back to the shop, she gave me a green malachite bracelet made of semi-precious stones to my exact taste. I was speechless. I immediately put it on my hand, but unfortunately, I managed to lose it when I was circling Kailash. I guess it protected me while on the pilgrimage, completed its task and has now left me to live its own life. That's how I consoled myself.

We had a few rather unpleasant surprises in Darchen. One young man from our group in his twenties got mountain sickness and had to stay behind. His parents also decided to cut their journey short and to take care of their son. Also, an unexpected notification arrived from China; the officials had decided at that point (probably temporarily) not to allow any pilgrims over 60 years old onto the mountain. So, those who qualified had to stay behind from the group as well and wait for us to return to Darchen.

Darchen, Tibet. Heli Grauberg, 2016

Mount Kailash. Heli Grauberg, 2016

Days 1 and 2 of the pilgrimage

DIRAPUK • CHARAN SPARSH (Tibet)

The first day of the pilgrimage – the journey to Dirapuk – was quite easy for me. Almost all the Indian women, and some of the men in our group, rented a horse, but it seemed only sensible for me to do the pilgrimage on foot. I was also reassured by my good helper, Umesh, the guide, who always had an oxygen tank in his backpack in case I needed extra oxygen. It's safe to say that I was fortunate not have to open it. Umesh also kept an eye on me to make sure I didn't accidentally step on the prayer flags. Once, while having a snack on the roadside, he quickly pulled me off the track before I got trampled by mighty 500 kg Tibetan yaks.

I didn't hire a porter (someone to carry my small backpack), but Umesh and I split the time carrying my things, and I paid him for the service instead. Usually, you automatically have to pay the local porter for three days, even if you only want a helper for a day. The same law was supposed to apply to horses. My roommate wanted to rent a horse (the horse is always accompanied) and carry her own backpack.

To make the circle of the Mount of Kailash, or kora, you must first pass the starting point of the pilgrimage to Yama Dwar (Yama is a death god and Dwar means door). Symbolically, this is how one renounces the mortal self and arrives as a pure being at the home of Lord Shiva - Mount Kailash, Tibet.

Pilgrim dog around Mount Kailash, Tibet.

Puja. Charan Sparsh, foot of Kailash, Tibet

Photos by Heli Grauberg, 2016

Puja. Charan Sparsh, foot of Kailash, Tibet.

Umesh Giri, 2016

This caused a problem; she was charged money for both the horse and a separate porter. Later, when we met at a teahouse, it turned out that my roommate had no idea where her backpack and porter were, but she would have liked to eat and drink water... Afterwards, I heard that porters often disappear for miles and then reappear as if from the ground. Drinking water, however, is an absolute must in the high mountains, and it's quite a shame when a baggage carrier who's been paid a hefty sum of money wanders off on his own. Porter services and horse rentals seem to be a really big business on the holy mountainside. Tibetans have a saying that doing the *kora* on a horse or yak is less valuable for a person, but good for the animal. Effort is worth extra points!

During my travels, I noticed a bird flying along with me and Umesh for a while, sometimes resting on the roadside or somewhere higher, but still watching us and flying next to us. Was it just curious, or was it some mystical occurrence of the holy place? I don't have an answer to that question...

Not everyone had a peaceful trip. My own roommate fell off the horse and had to take painkillers every day afterward. She was not the only one to fall.

There was an Indian woman in our group who was on this hike for the fourth time. Her health had deteriorated in the high-altitude conditions: incredible tiredness and an endless headache. She still decided to finish the pilgrimage victoriously – horses carried her around the mountain, and she fell right into her bed in the evenings. It was a mystery for her and the others why it went that way, when all the previous trips had gone just fine.

Finally, we reached our destination: Dirapuk, where as soon as we got to the guesthouse, we felt that Kailash was finally within our reach. We were so close. Right away, I pulled out my camera and began to capture photo after photo of this amazing view. The accommodations were traditional and simple. Some pilgrims had definitely already spent a few nights between those sheets – proof of that was some crusty sand and a strand of thick black hair. Fortunately, it was not a problem, because due to the cold, we slept in our outdoor clothes. There was no toilet in the guesthouse, so we had to go out in the field. There were no trees or even small hills to hide behind, but there was indeed an amazing view of the sacred mountain. It was a rather delicate situation, going to the toilet in the moonlight and coming across a businessman from our group, but one can get used to anything. Truthfully, this was the only accommodation where there was no toilet. I really recommend that women wear a longer tunic over their pants, because during the pilgrimage, you often have to do your business behind the tiniest hill or bush. Of course, if you drink a little less fluid, you can hold it till you can access the outdoor toilets at pilgrimage resting spots.

Usually, you rest only one night in Dirapuk before going on the pilgrimage the next day. The guide and I had to act according to the group's plans, because we belonged with them now. So, we took an additional day in Dirapuk to go to the foot of Mount Kailash, an opportunity I hadn't even allowed myself to dream of. After a couple of kilometres walk and a climb up the slippery rocks, we were met with a powerful stony toe, or maybe the toe of a shoe coming from the ice wall, depending on who saw it. *Charan* means feet and *Sprash* means touch. According to a Hindi tradition, anyone who touches an elder's feet gets blessed, and their ego suppressed. It's a sign of great respect. Touching Kailash's foot is supposed to be equal to touching Shiva's feet. Thank God for the Chinese rules, which led me to this exact group. It was a fantastic experience to be so close to the holy mountain and participate in the ceremony called *puja*, held according to Indian traditions, for which you need water, incense, candles and a bell. By chanting mantras, you appeal to different gods, as if calling them down to Earth. You put *prasada* (food and water offered to a deity during worship) on the altar, which you can eat after the blessing. Prayers were sent on their way to get the gods blessing on the pilgrimage and on all of life. Unfortunately, only a few group members headed to Charan Sparsh on foot, because most of them didn't want to tire themselves before the next day of pilgrimage, which would be the most difficult.

Our group had its own kitchen team, consisting of mainly Sherpas and guides. Tasty Indian dishes were prepared three times a day. Indian cuisine was chosen because the whole group consisted of Hindus, with the exception of one Estonian. Dinner was unusually late for me, and the Sherpas often brought the food to our beds, so we could fall asleep right after the meal. On the mornings of the pilgrimage, the food was packed to go – in addition to salty snacks, we had some fruits and chocolate

Pilgrimage around Mount Kailash. Horsemen in the early morning.

Day 3 of pilgrimage

DOLMA LA PASS • GAURI KUND • ZUTULPUK (Tibet)

The early morning of day three was the hardest part of the hike: we trekked from Dirapuk to Zutulpuk. This section is usually done on the second day of pilgrimage, but we spent an additional day in Dirapuk. I felt the height a bit – it was hard to breathe. There was also much more climbing and descending than on the first day. The guides and Sherpas whispered in secret that six pilgrims had already met their sad end there in recent days.

Om Namah Shivaya, Om Namah Shivaya, Om Namah Shivaya… Teacher Yogiraj Gurunath Siddhanath asked me to chant this Hindi mantra during my entire pilgrimage. I did this dutifully and hoped for the protection of Shiva. I remembered when, years ago, Gurunath, from whom I've received much wise spiritual guidance and teachings during the years, turned right to me in an Indian ashram and said: "You know, why you are here?! You practised yoga in your previous life!" I guess it's supposed to be like that; if you did yoga in your previous life, you would continue where you had left off the last time. Interesting, interesting… Have I been on Mount Kailash pilgrimages in my previous lives, and that is why I keep wanting to come back to this 52-kilometer circle?

Many pilgrims around Mount Kailash carry and spin the prayer wheels, sending good and sacred thoughts on the road. The prayers put into the turning mill are supposed to bring instant good karma, according to the Buddhist beliefs, and so does the repeated oral mantra. Everywhere you look, prayer flags flutter in the wind and small stone cairns mark the expressed prayers. The prayer flag tradition dates back to the pre-Buddhist era and its colours always are yellow (earth), green (water), red (fire), white (air) and blue (space).

Burly yaks carry huge loads in the harsh high-altitude conditions around Mount Kailash, and life is not easy for them, as the pilgrims' bags are packed with an endless variety of necessities (portable kitchen equipment, drinking water bottles and other stuff).

On the road I met the same Indian guys I met in Hilsa. They were dressed even more nicely and looked important, sitting on their horses. I remembered the great preparations and training that they had been talking about doing before the trip.... but I guess they felt more confident on horseback.

On our third day (usually second day for pilgrims) of the pilgrimage, we crossed the trip's culmination, the highest place – 5,630 meters above sea level – Dolma La Pass. Passing the place full of waving prayer flags and things pilgrims had sacrificed is supposed to symbolise a rebirth for a person. For Hindus, it's a joy to die in this highest point, because they are so close to Shiva at that moment.

From close by, it was possible to catch a glimpse of the green waters of the holy Gauri Kund Lake. According to Hindu mythology, the god Shiva's wife, Parvati, was washing herself in the lake when she decided to give life to her son, the deity Ganesha, moulding him from soap foam. She put her precious son to keep watch so that no one would interrupt her bathing. The god Shiva returned unexpectedly from his travels and saw a strange boy at the entrance who would not let him see his wife. He became terribly angry and cut off Ganesha's head. When the goddess Parvati saw this, her grief was great, and she asked Shiva to bring the boy back to life. The god Shiva brought the head of the first living creature he saw, an elephant. He placed it on the boy's shoulders, and soon Ganesha was alive again. In Hinduism, the elephant-headed deity Ganesha is very popular – the remover of obstacles, the god of wisdom and good fortune. All good deeds and ceremonies begin with a prayer to him. His large head represents wisdom.

Going down to the emerald-green lake is not that easy, because it's at the bottom of a rather deep slope. Thankfully, our guides collected some water themselves, and I also carried this nectar home with me, gradually drinking it. According to belief, spraying with Gauri Kund water will clean your mind and soul. The water is a perfect tool for purification rituals.

At the tourist office, Krishna had handed me a trekking pole I was supposed to carry around with me until we got to a terribly deep descent near Dolma La Pass. Without the stick, I probably would have flown down there headfirst. Now, I thanked Krishna in my heart.

On all Kailash pilgrimage circle days, Umesh and I took snack breaks and some other small resting breaks. In addition to the food packs packed by our cooks, I had chocolate and nuts, which were supposed to provide additional energy and which I often snacked on.

The guide and I were in a such rush that we passed all the men in our group, who were also doing the circle by foot. Pilgrimage should not be an athletic effort, but I just love to walk fast and wanted to finish the circle that day so I could rest a bit and deal with other stuff. Closer to the evening, when we reached the Zutulpuk guesthouse, I had enough energy to go wander around alone, get acquainted with the surroundings and take some photos. I managed to capture pictures of a rabbit and a local cave animal, a marmot, and when I finally collapsed into my bed, I slept great, despite not having washed or changed out of my travel clothes.

Marmot around Mount Kailash, Tibet.

Gauri Kund, Tibet. According to Hindi mythology, Shiva's wife Parvati was bathing in this lake when she decided to give life to the deity called Ganesha.

Highest peak of the camp, 5630 m, Dolma La Pass, Tibet. Guide Umesh & Heli.

Descending Dolma La Pass, Tibet.

3x Heli Grauberg, 2016

Last, 4th day of the pilgrimage

ZUTULPUK • DARCHEN (Tibet)

We were once again woken early in the morning to complete the last part of the outer circle of the pilgrimage around Mount Kailash. To be completely honest, it was the easiest part of the hike. It required no special effort to finish those last kilometres on a smooth dusty road. Of course, I felt the high altitude and couldn't exactly run, nor could I talk too fast or too eagerly. At the end of the pilgrimage, the horses that had just been dismounted stood close together and rested their feet. At the end, our group's bus was waiting to move on to the point that marked both the beginning and the end, the village of Darchen, to collect our travel bags from the guesthouse, where we had left them. On the Kailash circuit, the small backpack was all we needed for three or four days. We were also joined in Darchen by members of the group who had stayed behind: a son, now recovered from his health problems, and his parents, and a couple of pilgrims in their 60s, whom China had prohibited from going to the mountain because of their age.

We were blessed with amazing weather. It made the whole pilgrimage way easier. On the road, I needed just a warm one-layer jacket; wearing even a hoodie under it was too much.

Final stop of the kora, Tibet.

Lake Manasarovar, Mount Kailash across the lake, Tibet.

2x Heli Grauberg, 2016

"Lucky coin" from Lake Manasarovar and the nighttime nightmare

LAKE MANASAROVAR (Tibet)

Lake Manasarovar, with a perimeter of approximately 100 kilometres, is thought to be an embodiment of positivity and cleanliness. Vast, round, and full of blue-green water, this lake is located more than 4000 meters above sea level and is the highest freshwater lake in the world. It is several tens of kilometres southeast of Kailash. Only a few very dedicated pilgrims make the circle around the lake by foot. On our way back from Mount Kailash we did the *kora* around sacred Lake Manasarovar by bus. Hindus believe that the lake was formed from the minds of the god Brahma and that Shiva, transformed into a swan, swims on it. Hindus believe that drinking from the lake and immersing yourself in it frees you of all sins and opens a direct path to Lord Shiva after death. Nevertheless, Tibetans avoid going in the water for fear of polluting it.

I put on a summer dress for the lake and dove headlong into the water at the appointed place. The first dive is supposed to be for yourself, the second for your ancestors and the third for gurus, or teachers. After that, you can make as many dips or sacrifices for as many people as you please. We filled our bottles with water to take them home with us, and after all the chores, our group performed *havan,* a traditional Indian fire ceremony where mantras are recited, various deities and forces of nature are invoked, offerings are made to the fire, and blessings and solutions to life's problems are requested. And, oh! Wonder of wonders, four swans suddenly appeared on the completely empty and smooth lake. Intuition suggested that they were the god Shiva with his wife Parvati and children Ganesha and Murugan.

Right there, during *havan,* one member of our group found a coin from Lake Manasarovar and truly believed it to be a lucky coin that must be passed on. For some reason, they chose me. I couldn't help but think that this coin didn't appear out of thin air; somebody threw it there for some reason, but to be polite, I put it in my wallet and forgot about the story.

We spent our night in a guesthouse near the lake. An unexpected nightmare woke me up in the middle of the night. I had never experienced it, only seen it in a paranormal TV program called "A Haunting".

Our guesthouse with the watch tower and visiting place of the nightmare.

2x Heli Grauberg, 2016

*Thunder.
Lake Manasarovar,
Tibet.*

When I woke up, my first thought was that somebody had died in the guesthouse room and the spirit hadn't found peace. I truly hoped it was not real and wanted to go back to sleep, but that was out of the question – somebody physically attacked me. Someone pressed on me and bent my hand against the bed with great force, as if they were pulling the back of my hand with their nails. It was so real I was afraid to fall asleep. Suddenly I thought of that stranger's coin in my wallet. I dressed in the middle of the night and went to Lake Manasarovar all alone, lighting my path with a flashlight, and threw that coin back into the water. It could be a lucky coin with someone's wishes, but somebody may have also tried to throw away bad karma with this coin. It was pitch black outside by the lake and, thanks to this small mantra chant, I suddenly realised I was not alone. Probably some pilgrims had made a camp by the lake to observe the nightly bathing of the gods. Human eyes are thought to be able to see those pretty, luminous, radiant flashes of light above the water between three and five in the morning. It's also called the time of Brahma Muhurta, which falls approximately 1.5 hours before the sunrise – the creator's hour. It's also a very good time to do yoga and other mental practices (the time of sunrise varies depending on the season and location). The mystical, heavenly dance on Lake Manasarovar – flashes change in size and colour, approach and retreat. In reality, everything has been filmed and examined, but they haven't found any scientific evidence up to this day.

I had set an alarm with my roommates for this event earlier and I had one hour left to sleep. So I headed to our guesthouse when, suddenly, a very tall man quietly stepped up next to me without speaking. I had a very small flashlight in my hands, and he took advantage of my light to find his way. I don't know if he was young or old, local or a tourist, perhaps an alien? I was afraid to shine the light onto the figure, so we walked towards my guesthouse together. The path shared with the stranger wasn't long, but it seemed endless. Would he talk? Come to the guesthouse? Was he planning to do something to me? Finally, a bit shyly, I turned down at the bend in the road, and the tall man silently walked on, away into the pitch black…

Back in my room, I fell asleep quickly; there were no further problems with the nightmare. About an hour later, I got to wake up again and go to a special watchtower with my roommates. The weather was bad, and unfortunately, we missed the gods dance on the lake. So soon enough we went back to dreamland (I guess this was a night without a miracle).

Famous Indian yogi and writer Sadhguru has repeatedly taken the path to Mount Kailash and Lake Manasarovar in Tibet with his students. In his experience, the most active time on the lake is at night between 2:30 and 3:45 AM. The predominant colour on the holy water during this unexplained phenomenon is electric blue. This guru says that the aura of everyone who has followed the path of yoga and done certain yoga practices turns to blue – electric blue. Everything that happens on Lake Manasarovar is difficult to put in words and explain logically. Sadhguru says: "It's life, but not as we know it."

Sadhguru describes the time of Brahma Muhurta as a special one, a time that offers the opportunity to be sort of a "creator" yourself. It's the last quarter of the night when the planet's relationship with the sun and the moon impacts the individual, and physiological changes take place in the human system (it's scientifically proven that even the quality of urine changes during this period). It's exactly the time of Brahma Muhurta when the pineal gland in our midbrain produces the highest amount of melatonin, putting us in a relaxed state that yogis use to their advantage in this early practising hour. Sadhguru has said that the best time to get up and practise yoga is three-thirty in the morning. This is a way to gain the most from this special creator's hour for mental development. This early hour, though, is said to be really useful only to those practitioners who have gotten their initiation straight from the teacher, or guru (information isha.sadhguru.org).

Havan and our group. Lake Manasarovar, Tibet. Umesh Giri, 2016

Lake Manasarovar, Tibet.

Heli Grauberg, 2016

Glance on the Demonic Lake Rakshastal

LAKE RAKSHASTAL (Tibet)

We also stayed 3.7 kilometres from Lake Manasarovar, by the crescent shaped Lake Rakshastal (Devil's Lake) in the west, where you honour the body of water only with your glance; no other contact is made. In contrast to Lake Manasarovar, that lives its life to the fullest, Lake Rakshastal, with its salty water, is lifeless; neither water plants nor fish live there.

Hindu mythology says that it is an enchanted lake, a home to the ten-headed demon king Ravana. Despite its infamy, the lake is no less lovely than any other water body in Tibet.

The narrow river Ganga Chhu runs between Lakes Manasarovar and Rakshastal and, according to Hindu mythology, was founded by ancient Hindi wisemen (*rishis*) to carry clean water into the demonic lake.

Lake Rakshastal, aka Devil's Lake, Tibet. The saltwater lake Rakshastal is lifeless and has no water plants, nor fish.

Heli Grauberg, 2016

Back to Hilsa and waiting several nights and days for a helicopter

HILSA (Nepal)

The road back to the village Hilsa, on the border of China and Nepal, greeted us with bad weather. The helicopters couldn't take off for two to three days. So I had to spend two more nights in the Nepali village, where Umesh helped me find lodging in a home for an extra fee. I sat with the family in the kitchen till late at night and observed their evening activities. I ate well and got a taste of homemade cider. Umesh took me to the homes of this tiny village; they were like temporary cafes, where one could sit and buy bottled beer and snacks. In one home, they were in the middle of boiling strong spirits, called *rakshi,* in a huge pot.

Nobody knew how long the weather would tease us. Once, Umesh had waited for a week for a helicopter to get to a Nepali town (also called a village), Simikot. Many pilgrims were in a really bad mood: I saw angry people, yelling, with tears in their eyes. Due to bad weather, I had to call Krishna and ask him to help me change my plane tickets for the route from Kathmandu to London. I knew that nothing depends on me, so I was as peaceful as could be and enjoyed the extra days in the mountains given to me. I felt carefree, despite the fact my budget had been blown a long time ago and my vacation from work was coming to an end. I guess peace of mind was the aftermath of the pilgrimage…

Finally, the wind stopped, and helicopters started buzzing between Hilsa and Simikot like bees among the spring flowers – one came and another went. The aircrafts were filled with as many people as possible. No thought was spared for safety rules. Everybody wanted to go home, and as soon as possible!

Helicopter landing. Hilsa, Nepal

Donkeys in Hilsa, Nepal

Donkeys curious about the guesthouse in Hilsa, Nepal.

3x Heli Grauberg, 2016

In the middle of the runway at Simikot, waiting for a flight back

SIMIKOT (Nepal)

After a short helicopter flight over the beautiful Nepali mountain range, I landed in the Simikot airport to get the next flight to Nepalgunj. Many people had been stuck because of the weather, and I got news that it would take at least two to three days to travel further. By this time, I was completely alone and very eager to go back home, so I wasn't exactly happy about this information. I was passing the time with other pilgrims in the middle of the runway, where I had just landed on the helicopter, and I decided not to leave. Luckily, Umesh arrived soon enough with some people that I knew. After some time, I had a strong urge to go to the toilet, and I definitely did not want to go inside the terminal, because I was not sure I could get back on the runway without impediments. I was in the middle of the runway and ready to jump on the plane any minute. There was an incredibly stinky dry toilet next to the runway with two open walls, full of faeces, that anybody could glance into. There were a number of Nepali male aviation enthusiasts on the other side of the wire mesh, and I lost all sense of shame.

Suddenly, I saw a familiar face from the day I had arrived in Simikot from Nepalgunji – I saw the same guy who had helped me with my accommodations. I begged him to arrange a flight for me right then. There wasn't much hope, but after a phone call to Krishna and I don't know who else, I sat myself down in a seat on a plane soon enough. Krishna again! It was the last time I would see my guide, Umesh, on this trip. I later learned that our guides and Sherpas didn't get on any flight, so they had to take a several-day long troublesome and tiring trip by land.

Simikot airport, Nepal.
Heli Grauberg, 2016

Miracle plane flight from Nepalgunj

NEPALGUNJI (Nepal)

When I got to Nepalgunji I was forewarned that the flights were so full that there was only a slight hope of getting to Kathmandu in the near future. I found the right person from the airport, whose name was given to me by Krishna as a contact person. The man said that there might be an open seat on the plane outside waiting to take off, so I should wait. And again, Krishna pulled off a miracle! The plane was held for a minute, and I was registered on the flight on the last second. I ran to the packed plane to reach the capital, Kathmandu. Ugh, what a relief and a joy to finally sit there among men in white shirts. Despite the fact that I might have been just a bit stinky, and my face and neck were covered with dust.

Back to Kathmandu and a trip back home

KATHMANDU (Nepal)

I landed in Kathmandu in a downpour – it was monsoon season. It was already dark outside, and I had to find a taxi from the airport with my bags. I trudged between people to get a ride to my hotel in the centre of the city, where my suitcase and room were waiting for me. I didn't have any more local Nepali money, but fortunately, I was able to make a deal with the taxi driver – we called Krishna, who explained the situation, and I paid for the taxi the next day. When I got to my hotel, I took a shower right away to get rid of all the dirt. Sand was stuck on my neck, and with my dirty, dusty hair, I was the picture of a true dust monster. All I was missing was a pair of horns. After cleaning up, I went out, hoping to find a bite to eat, but for that I needed money. Unfortunately, all the nearby banks were already closed, and I couldn't withdraw any cash. So, I decided to go to sleep, although I could have paid with my card in many restaurants.

Because I had to change my flight due to the helicopter problems and the trip got extended, the travel package from Krishna's travel agency had ended, so I had to pay extra for every additional night at the hotel. The next morning, I got my suitcase and other stuff and moved to the Kathmandu Guest House, located on the same street, where I had stopped on my earlier stops. This guesthouse had a varying price range – from more expensive to cheaper. It was nice and clean and had a luscious green garden with a cafeteria, a swing and statues. I spent my next three nights there. I shopped during the day and enjoyed my evenings among the locals of the Thamel district (where the hotel was located). On my last day, Krishna sent a taxi to pick me up and transport me to the airport. In the airport, I placed my suitcase and backpack in the security control line and, surprise! – the airport security had loads of questions: "What bottles are those?". I answered that these are seven plastic bottles with holy water. "What are you doing with this holy water?" they asked. "I use them for rituals," I answered. "Where is it from?" I took out the bottles and realised that people like me are a form of entertainment for them. I also found out the reason – Western people usually don't have a bag full of holy water. I didn't mention that I was planning to take all this – crystal clear water from Lake Manasarovar, snow water dripping from the foothills of Charan Sparsh and nectar fished out of the birthplace of Lord Ganesha, Gauri Kund– and drink it all at home. And I did!

Epilogue for Part I

Dear reader, I was not sure if this Mount Kailash trip would continue from here… It was in January of 2019 when Krishna sent me an e-mail announcing that his Nepalese travel agency was organising just one inner circle (*inner kora*) pilgrimage in 2019, and I was kindly invited to join if I'd like. Knowing that getting a permit to this region was unlikely anyway, I decided to wait and see. I sent 300 US dollars as an advance payment through Western Union and started saving money for this trip. Would Krishna really able to negotiate with China for a permit for me, a foreigner, to enter the *inner kora* region when, according to what they were saying, it was forbidden to enter the area? So, my dream could actually come true? You never know, Krishna…

Mount Kailash in the foamy clouds.

Uploading my travel pictures to the computer in the Kathmandu Guest House, Nepal.

2x Heli Grauberg, 2016

कैलास

PILGRIMAGE TO MOUNT KAILASH 2019

10th of July – 29 of July

TRANSPORT **ACCOMODATION**
buses   hotels
SUV   hostels
   guesthouses

LONDON
United Kingdom

KATHMANDU
Nepal

RASUWAGADHI
Nepalese and Chinese border

KYIRONG
Tibet

SAGA
Tibet

LAKE MANASAROVAR
Tibet

DARCHEN
Tibet

DIRAPUK
Tibet

ZUTULPUK
Tibet

DARCHEN
Tibet

PART II

Decision to go on a new pilgrimage

Unfortunately, this was not what I had secretly hoped for – not all of our group got a permit from the Chinese to enter the paths of the Kailash *inner kora*. So, it was not that I was a foreigner; it was the safety of the people that was important – to save people's lives, the permit for the inner circle is not given out so easily. At the same time, I found out through social media that those paths were still being walked even in 2019.

Krishna and I had an agreement that if I did not get a permit to the inner circle, he would return the deposit I'd paid to the agency in January. To go or not to go? I had lived for half a year under the star of the Kailash pilgrimage, and it was hard to give up the thought now. An additional bonus was the knowledge that my very good friend Maria wished to join me on my trip to Mount Kailash this time.

I got acquainted with Maria through Annika Allikmäe (Nõmberg) through special yoga lessons in Tallinn, Estonia. I am grateful to Annika for being the first teacher to ignite my passion for the ancient yoga world. Thanks to her, I am still on that path. Our yoga lessons were not just hatha yoga poses. Annika shared her Teacher Ishwarananda's knowledge of the techniques of reorganising the person's inner world, told us about healthy nutrition and generally shared lots of important knowledge on how to raise our quality of life. We also focused on yoga therapy – freeing the physical body of pain, sickness and overall stress. We wrote down all the information gotten from the yoga lessons and now, more than ten years later, those notebooks still sit on my nightstand.

Maria and I had a mutual feeling of kinship from the start, and the friendship has lasted. It has taken us on India trips and other fun joint adventures.

The initial Tibetan plan was as follows: Maria would join the group to Mount Kailash and later, when the group was on the paths of *inner kora*, Maria could join some outer circle (*outer kora*) pilgrims from another group. Maria would have completed the outer circle and I the inner circle, and later we would meet in the Darchen village again to begin our journey back to Nepal together. Humans make plans, and God laughs…

I still felt a secret call back to the holy mountain, so I listened to it and sent a travel confirmation e-mail to Krishna. The new plan was to make the same traditional 52- kilometre circle around Mount

Kailash that I'd done in 2016, but to reach Tibet via highways, not by air. Krishna planned our trip, and based on earlier experience, I trusted him without reservation.

The name Krishna is beloved in both Nepal and India, so it's used widely. "Hindu god Krishna is the embodiment of divine happiness and love, he destroys all the disadvantages and pain. He is the protector of sacred sayings and sacred cows. He is a trickster, lover and the source of all knowledge" – that is what is written on the Lilleoru home page about Lord Krishna.

I don't know if the tourist agency owner Krisha has all those traits, but he is doing good at his job. Oh, and he mentioned to me that he belongs to the highest Nepali caste – the caste of *brahmins* (priests and teachers). It's a very important fact in their culture; for me, it's just a piece of interesting information.

Krishna Dhakal. Owner of Kathmandu Holiday Tours & Travels.
Backround: Potala palace in the capital of Tibet, Lhasa.
Krishna's private collection, 2019

Horsemen riding. Pilgrimage around Mount Kailash, Tibet.

Heli Grauberg, 2016

Asking for blessings for my pilgrimage at the Shiva *havan* fire ceremony at Lilleoru

1/07/19, Monday – Just before my second pilgrimage to Kailash, I visited the Lilleoru centre in Estonia. On the first of July, it holds a *havan* dedicated to Shiva. Shiva is the initial source of everything that exists and is the one who gives yoga knowledge to people. It was the time and place to ask blessings for our trip to Kailash. The evening before, Merike and I had agreed that we would drive to the *havan* together. Merike is one of the pujari's at Lilleoru who performs *arti* (light ceremonies) and *havan* (fire ceremonies) with the recitation of mantras. Additionally, she is now a professional teacher of *veda* mantras and, most importantly, a sweet person. We arrived with Merike early in the morning, before six. I went to the kitchen, where I got myself a coconut, which I had beautifully decorated with a red ribbon and freshly picked flowers. Merike was already ready to put a *chandan* on everyone's forehead including mine. It's supposed to help you focus your thoughts and protect you. As a thanks for the upcoming ceremony, I left a donation in the box in the kitchen and quickly ran outside. The weather was amazingly warm. I threw off my trainers and did three rounds around the white temple, barefoot in the morning dew. I visited the bull, Nandi, and reached the Lilleoru stone circle, the oldest sanctuary there. At six o' clock, I sat with the other arrivals around the fireplace, or *dhun,* under an open roof. The *havan* was about to begin, held by Teacher Ingvar (Ishwarananda) and Merike. I really hope and truly believe that Shiva's good blessings reached us all.

Once, when singing mantras around the living fire during the yoga initiation at Lilleoru, natural forces showed me a true miracle! Rain was pouring in the nearby forest thicket, but some metres in front of the fireplace roof, the rain stopped as if cut with a knife, and we enjoyed dry weather. I wanted to film it, but unfortunately, I did not have my phone in my pocket…

On their website, Ingvar Villido speaks about *havan:* "To recreate balance and hold it between the individual and their surroundings, ancient wisemen created plenty of different techniques. One of them was the fire ceremony, aka *yagya* (havan). Those ancient wisemen felt in detail how all the seen and unseen world works and based on this feeling, they created a detailed action plan, so people could contact those creative forces and get help.

The fireplace is the focus of the fire ceremony, and through fire, you contact the other side. Let's say it's the unseen world; for some, it is the spiritual world. But there, on the invisible side, are all the forces that our visible life consists of and comes from.

For the participant, the fire ceremony is an opportunity to free yourself from harm and to ask blessings, so your endeavours will go smoothly. Harmful things can be removed from one's life. Mantras are chanted throughout the ceremony; that means turning to different facets, or natural forces, and offerings are brought to the fire that consist of different products (cereal, flowers, *ghee*, etc.). Every one of them is a symbol – something you transfer from the inner world to the outer. Fire eats everything it touches and the only thing left is ashes. As a result of the purification, something is revealed: something that does not burn and is eternal – pure consciousness, like an endless room containing everything. The human's true identity is here, not in the things that we usually identify ourselves with."

I later learned that Ingvar received the dedication to perform such ceremonies in 2002 from Shri Muniraj, the chief disciple and ashram leader of the Indian saint Mahavatar Haidakhan Babaji. In the book *Stories of Conscious Change*, Ingvar recalls, "Shri Muniraj, my initiator into these sciences, from whom I also received my second spiritual name (the first was given to me during a Buddhist retreat), lay down conditions - to obtain permission to perform fire ceremonies, the place must be made available for public use. Perhaps obtaining the permit required not only learning but donating my privately owned property for public use."

The NGO brings together a core group of Ingvar's students, which now includes more than 170 people, and of course the centre itself has grown, offering both public training and in-depth *kriya* yoga classes. It's a bit unbelievable that an ashram of such profound teachings, spiritually named Sat Chit Agastishwarar Gurukkulam, can be found so far from India.

The Maha Munindra temple, Lilleoru, Estonia.

Winter by Jüri Joost

Summer by Aimar Säärits

Flower of Life, Lilleoru, Estonia. Jüri Joost

An eye-shaped lake Amrita, Lilleoru, Estonia. Jüri Joost

Kali's gate and bull Nandi, Lilleoru, Estonia. Kai Laanmets

The Ishwara temple, Lilleoru, Estonia. Jüri Joost

Arrival in Nepal

KATHMANDU (Nepal)

11/07/19 Thursday – Kathmandu, warm and slightly humid as it is during the monsoon season, greeted us with open arms this time. I had the honour of stepping onto this land of magnificent mountains for the fourth time; it was Maria's second time. It seems as if Nepal is trying to go electronic, because all the visa applications have to be personally filled out through a screen system on the registration machine. There are several of those machines, but a long queue was still inevitable. We saw that all the passengers had problems entering the data into the machine. The passport information should have been entered automatically if you placed the document under a certain place on the screen, but for some reason, the thing did not work, and most of the people had to enter the passport data and other necessary information for the visa manually. You could also take an automatic photo for the visa on this machine and there was a separate table to pay the official 40 USD for a 30-day visa (2019 rate). It took some time, but we got it done. Finally, we marched proudly through the border point – we were very tired from the nightly flight, but also excited about the upcoming adventure. The whole visa procedure, including retrieving our luggage, took about an hour. Krishna's brother, Raj, who came to meet us, was waiting for us with the driver.

The driver first took us to the Kathmandu Guesthouse, which had become one of my favourite hotels in Nepal, mostly because of the amazing garden and lovely breakfast served in this verdant garden. It's a wonderful little oasis in the rush of bustling Kathmandu and Thamel. A small standard room is not ideal, neither is it cheap, but a garden that resembles a paradise on earth more than makes up for it. And how much does one sit in their room during a trip, anyway? Many famous people have stayed in this hotel; for example, George Harrison of The Beatles stayed here in the seventies, as did the creators of *Lonely Planet*, Tony and Maureen Wheeler. Over the years, many other famous people have found temporary shelter here. Unfortunately, this building was not spared during the terrifying 2015 Nepalese earthquake; it suffered damage, so one wing was closed for extensive renovations.

We threw our suitcases in our hotel room and ran to a photo booth a few steps further to take pictures for the Chinese visa and to get a Nepali pre-paid phone card. Not having slept a wink after the overnight plane ride, unwashed and without make-up, we pushed our hair behind our ears for the photographers, to look at least a bit better. As soon as we'd clicked and the pictures were ready, Krishna's brother grabbed the still-hot photos from our hands and disappeared into the maze of Thamel's dusty streets.

Maria and I finished our short day at the New Orleans Cafe, a stone's throw from the Kathmandu Guest House.

Excursion to the Manakamana temple

KATHMANDU • MANAKAMANA (Nepal)

12/07/19, Friday – There was a complete downpour during the night, but that is typical during the rainy season in Nepal. The night before, we had booked a car and driver through Krishna's company for a morning drive to Manakamana temple, located about 3–4 hours (just over 100 km) from Kathmandu. The shrine is dedicated to the Hindu goddess Bhagwati. *Mana* means heart, and *kamana* means desire. It is a well-known fact that the goddess Manakamana grants the wishes of all who enter the temple and offer anything – fruit, flowers, rice, incense, goats, chickens, etc. – to the temple. Buddhists, Hindus and ordinary tourists alike go to the goddess to receive blessings, and that's what we planned to do.

As planned, Maria and I were waiting for the driver at eight in the morning in the hotel lobby. After a 15-minute wait, we sent an SMS cry for help to Raj: "There's still no car!" Raj jumped on his scooter and rushed to our hotel to figure out what the deal was. Because of the bad weather conditions, our driver was 30 minutes late, and I couldn't imagine that Raj himself would arrive in response to the SMS.

Manakamana, with its famous sanctuary, is high up on the mountain (1,302 m) and can be reached via a 15-minute ride in Nepal's one-of-a-kind cable car. Foreigners have to pay 20 USD for this ride. Goats and other smaller farm animals, like chickens, are sacrificed near the temple. There were a few goats on leashes, waiting... On certain days of the festival, there is a lot of blood flowing because there is non-stop sacrifice. It's also a place where ritual bells are rung and mantras are chanted throughout the day. And it's also the place to get the sweet smell of incense in your nostrils and in your hair.

Before the cable car was installed, it took 3–4 hours to get from the old village to the shrine, and pilgrims had to negotiate the steep path up the hill. The slippery and muddy roads during the rainy seasons did not scare anyone, and every year, large numbers of people make the arduous journey to receive the blessings of the wish granter, Manakamana. Due to poor accessibility, however, the elderly and pilgrims with physical disabilities could only dream of visiting the Manakamana temple until 1998, when the cable car was ready. This project came true thanks to a businessman named Shrestha. Born in Gorkha, he came up with the idea in cooperation with Austrian developers of cable cars, who had built lots of analogues around the world. Gorgeous glass cabins for passengers glide up the hill, and there are more robust metal vehicles for cargo and sacrificial animals. Only a one-way charge for the goats... How beautiful it was to fly in a glass cabin over a valley, seeing it rush by, and a little flowing river, and all through a wild downpour. On a clear day, you could find yourself gliding above the creamy white clouds in the heights up there.

In 2011, when I visited Manakamana for the first time, I also had to deal with a heavy downpour. The narrow streets had become a creek, and you couldn't pass without getting your feet wet. Village dogs pushed themselves against each other playfully, trying to get some shade under the roof. On a temple wall we saw a sign saying: "No entry for non-Hindus". So all I could do in this downpour was to walk around the sanctuary, hide in a café and then go ahead to my lodging. The next morning, there was no more sign of the rain; the sky was completely clear. I was walking alone in the early morning light along the narrow streets of Manakamana towards the holy temple and — oh! What a wonder – there was a breathtaking sight next to the temple: a panorama of the snow-capped peaks of the Himalayas - the Annapurna range, the Himalchuli and Manaslu mountains, and the clouds below, perfecting the view. The majestic mountains were so close, and I felt as if I had suddenly stepped into a real fairy tale. It was a sight to remember for a lifetime. I ran back to the lodge and woke up my partner so that he too could take in the morning beauty. When we arrived the previous rainy day, we had no idea that anything so beautiful could ever be experienced in that village. In 2019, Maria and I missed out on the mountain views and creamy white clouds because of the downpour. If I hadn't seen this amazing view on my previous trip, I wouldn't have known what I'd missed.

View from the Manakamana temple of the snowy peaks of the Himalayas on the morning of the 2011 trip, Nepal.

Heli Grauberg, 2011

Granter of all wishes, Manakamana temple in the downpour, Nepal, 2019.

On the way to the granter of all wishes – Manakamana temple, Nepal.

Sacrificial flowers for the Manakamana temple on sale.

Air ride with the cable car. On our way to the granter of all wishes, Manakamana temple, Nepal.

Dogs sheltering from the rain under the Manakamana cable cars.

On our way to the granter of all wishes, Manakamana temple.

Nepali dish in the cafeteria near the Manakamana temple.

Photos by Heli Grauberg, 2019

Manakamana temple and the houses nearby were not spared during the 2015 earthquake and were also badly damaged. By now, everything has been renovated and there is no sign of the damage. All the buildings had been rebuilt. The warning sign on the temple was also gone: "No entry for non-Hindus". To test it, Maria and I stepped through the gate of the sanctuary's garden and passed the guarding soldiers. First, one uniformed man instructed us to leave our shoes behind the gate in the downpour – it was a sure sign of us getting into the Manakamana temple to ask for our wishes to be granted. And inside we were, and we both got our blessings from the local priest. A really small temple room was full of incense smoke. When we bowed before the priest, he asked our names and made red tilakas on our foreheads while chanting the mantras. Supposedly, he is a 17th-generation priest in this temple. There was a medium-sized pooch by the temple, chasing away the monkeys. The latter were trying to get into the sanctuary's garden and steal some tasty *prasad* (food offered to gods – bananas, apples etc.). The dog was so eager that we wondered if the temple had hired him or if he was a volunteer!

After the temple, we headed through the downpour to a local cafeteria, where we drank sweet tea with milk, or as locals call it, chai. Similar spiced chai with sweet milk is also offered in India, Pakistan and Tibet. This gingerbread-like spicy drink has fans all over the world. In the wider world it's known as chai (tea) latte. There are, of course, variations in how it is made – Asian masala chai is prepared with boiling tea leaves, spices, water and milk mix, while chai latte is made by adding spiced tea concentrate to whipped milk. The history of this traditional Indian beverage is thousands of years old, and the history of its discovery is the stuff of legend. The tea mixture, consisting of spices and herbs, is supposed to relieve stress and help with digestion. It also helps to warm the body and supposedly gives one strength to live. You can sense the influence of *dosha* (the Hindu healing system) in chai, where the combination of spices, herbs and sweeteners are used to treat illnesses.

We enjoyed this sweet and refreshing chai every day during our trip, both in Nepal and Tibet.

Almost every family in India, Nepal, Tibet, and even Bangladesh has their own *masala* tea recipe, that is, a particular combination of spices, milk, water and sugar.

Here is a recipe I have mixed myself, following the basics of making *chai masala:*

4 cups of water

1 cup of milk

2–3 teaspoons of black tea powder

6 teaspoons of sugar or honey

4 cloves
6 cardamoms pods
1,5g cinnamon bark (a stick as long as a finger)
Pinch of grated ginger
Pinch of black ground pepper

Boil 4 cups of water. Add 2-3 teaspoons of black tea powder to the boiling water and cover for 5 minutes on low heat. Next, add all the spices crushed in the mortar (cloves, cardamom, cinnamon peel - you can also leave some pieces in to bring out the flavours), grated ginger, pepper and sugar, and cook for about 5 minutes. Add one cup of milk while still on low heat, and boil the entire mixture for a few minutes.

Finally, simmer the liquid on low heat so that it thickens and the flavours are enhanced (I myself simmer for at least 20 minutes). During heating, the amount of *masala chai* is reduced, so I usually get 3.5–4 cups of *chai* from the amount I put in a pot. Sometimes I add no sugar at all; I just take the pot off the heat in the end and add honey to taste.

Pour the chai into a cup with the help of a filter and enjoy!

Masala chai pot with spices.
Shutterstock, TalyaAL

Visit to Boudhanath stupa and the house of the child goddess Kumari Ghar

KATHMANDU (Nepal)

13/07/19, Saturday – In the morning, we were woken up by a chorus of crows nesting in the garden of the Kathmandu Guest House – the note was taken up by one of the crows, followed by the choir cawing in response. Then another screechy lead singer, and another ear-scratching chorus. The concert lasted long enough to make us crawl out of bed in the early hours.

After a refreshing breakfast in the garden, Maria and I took the local bus and drove to the Boudhanath stupa. The bus ride was very colourful and noisy, but also very cheap. Every 30 seconds, the already crowded vehicle stopped to pick up more passengers. The bus driver was assisted by a very young boy, half of whose body was hanging outside the bus, shouting non-stop: "Boudhanath, Boudhanath!" People kept getting on, but luckily, they kept getting off, too.

Boudhanath complex is located about 6-7 kilometres from the Kathmandu centre, but the drive took a while. Compared to the rush of Kathmandu, it's a nice quiet place – stupa in the middle, surrounded by shops, cafes and temples. Movement around the stupa is clockwise, and the prayer mills in a row are also spun clockwise. There are always hundreds of people circling the stupa – humming mantras and rolling prayer beads in their palm. The prayer wheels around the base of the giant stupa are said to have the mantra *Om Mani Padme Hum* written on paper. The same text is also on the metal prayer wheels. Maria and I made many, many circles around the big stupa, which was like a meditative activity. You kept walking and walking and saying *Om Mani Padme Hum*.... It was also supposed to help get rid of bad karma and to purify your soul. There is a small temple in the northern part of the stupa, dedicated to the goddess, known as the protector and wish granter of the stupa. In the tiny temple, for a small fee, anyone can light a candle and make a wish.

We also visited Guru Lhakhang monastery next to the stupa, where monks sat in a row and gave as a chance to receive their blessings for a small donation.

We didn't want to pass up the opportunity; we entered. The monks read us mantras and we left with blessings and a yellow ribbon around our hand.

After all the rituals and blessings, it was time to get something to eat in a café. We found a nice place up on the terrace with a great view of the stupa. We ordered *momos,* a very popular local food.

These are small steamed pockets with vegetables (you can choose the filling) reminiscent of dumplings. We drank our favourite *chai* or tea with lots of sugar and milk, the flavours coming from different spices like cardamom, cinnamon, clove and ginger.

We headed back on the small, dusty, clacking bus again – it was interesting, and economical. When we got back to the centre, we headed to Turbar Square to see the house of Kumari Ghar. Of course, we hoped to see the living goddess Kumari in the window of her home. Dubar Squar, under the protection of UNESCO, is an old and beautiful district, with its temples dedicated to gods and royal palaces. Unfortunately, the square filled with magnificent buildings suffered much destruction in the 2015 earthquake. In 2019, many buildings were still in a rather miserable state, but the renovations were coming along.

We found the front of the Kumari's house filled with tourists, and we waited along with the others in a small garden patch for the goddess's appearance. Luck was not with me that day. Years ago, when Maria was sitting under the Kumari's window with her friend, they were surprised with an invitation to the goddess's room. Maria was fortunate enough to experience this kind of luck and blessing with her friend! No worries – maybe next time.

Popular dish, momos, in a café terrace near the Boudhanath stupa. Kathmandu, Nepal

Women taking care of the street dogs next to the Boudhanath stupa, Kathmandu, Nepal.

Bells next to the stupa, Kathmandu, Nepal.

Small temple near the Boudhanath stupa, Kathmandu, Nepal.

Photos by Heli Grauberg, 2019

My handmade silver jewellery in the expanses of Mount Kailash

KATHMANDU (Nepal)

14/07/19, Sunday — It was moving day. Maria and I packed all our suitcases and backpacks and lugged them through the streets of Thamel for 100 m until we got to a new, modern hotel called the Arts. Our Kailash pilgrimage package had officially begun.

We were standing in the Arts lobby when Umesh entered — we hadn't seen each other for three years. For some reason, the group assigned to him couldn't head to the mountain at the right time, so some of his pilgrims, including Umesh himself, had to join up with our group now. This was great news! After the 2016 pilgrimage, I had made silver Mount Kailash pendants at home as a thank you to Krishna and Umesh and sent them by parcel to Kathmandu. Using a special technique, I had pressed an imprint of a real photo of Mount Kailash into silver. When heated at high temperature, it became pure metal – 99.9% silver – and after careful polishing, it was quite nice and original. Umesh, seeing the same pendant hanging around my neck, announced with a slightly guilty expression that he had lost his jewellery on Mount Kailash. I said: "I'm so happy you lost it there!" I sincerely believe that the jewellery, created by my own hands with love, somewhere out there in the expanses of the City of the Gods, had brought me back to those paths.

In addition to the tourist office, Krishna also has a fast food restaurant where he invited Maria and me to have dinner with his friends, assistants and guides. It was interesting to talk to Krishna's friend, who had twice trekked up Everest, the highest mountain in the world, and now owns a mountaineering and trekking company in Nepal. We found out that a foreigner's permit to Everest costs 11,000 USD, but a Nepali only has to pay 700 USD. He had also met Westerners who had sold their houses back home to go on their dream trek – Everest. The issue of caste in Nepal also came up at the dinner table. In Nepal, it is possible to marry a partner from a different caste, but the woman then belongs to the husband's caste. It was a great evening, full of conversation and jokes, and later we headed off together to hear some jazz at the New Orleans Cafe.

Jewellry depicting Mount Kailash.

The tour begins! Visiting Budhanilkantha temple and Pashupatinath

KATHMANDU (Nepal)

15/07/19, Monday – The Arts Hotel alarm clock is a hatching dove with her partner right outside our window. One of them was neatly sitting on the eggs and was followed by constant noise – coo, coo, coo. Of course, the baby birds needed their parents' protection and care, so we enjoyed our companions.

The Kailash pilgrimage package was now in full swing, and we were taken on a day tour of the city by the travel agency. The first stop was at the Budhanilkantha temple in Kathmandu, dedicated to the god Vishnu, a benevolent Hindu deity tasked with preserving and protecting the world. A five-metre statue of Vishnu reclined in a voluminous pool, and we were all able to pass by it once and, if we wished, leave something as an offering. This lovely open-air temple was to be treasured by Hindus and Buddhists alike.

The whole group was then taken to the oldest and holiest temple complex of Pashupatinath, on the banks of the Bagmati River, where traditional cremation rituals take place. A white person can watch the burning ceremonies from a distance between the sacred buildings, but beware of the god Shiva, if peeping into the temple, where entry is forbidden to non-Hindus. As soon as we arrived at the Pashupatinath site, our group of Hindus got in right away, but Maria and I, tourist-looking Estonians, were asked for tickets. What else could we do but pay the entrance fee and enter the shrine, where we were followed by local activists who repeatedly reminded us that we had no business in the temple. I wonder why so many people cared?!! Had we tried to sneak past the ban and enter the shrine, we would surely have been literally torn to shreds at the temple door. It would probably have already happened in the long entrance queue to the temple, which we avoided, just in case. So, we just walked around. I paid a dollar to the sadhus for their permission to take their picture; we watched the smoke of a funeral pyre further away, we rested our feet among the holy women, we gazed at the temple complex and, finally, we found our guides to get back on the road.

About 15 minutes from the hotel, the tour bus had gotten into a small crash, so we had to walk to the hotel. We got caught in terrible traffic and, by the roadside, an electrical fire was being extinguished where millions of bundles of wires had caught fire.

In the evening, there was a briefing in the hotel's roof lounge. The travel agency owner, Krishna, along with his colleagues, introduced the Kailash pilgrimage itinerary and handed out small warm orange jackets, bigger travel bags and small backpacks with logos. There wasn't a jacket in my size, so I passed, but the bags were mandatory (we could keep all the souvenirs if we wished). Pilgrims keep their belongings in the larger numbered bags for the whole trip, and in the village of Darchen, near Kailash, they are left at the hotel for three days and replaced with small backpacks provided by the company.

Maria and I had arrived in Kathmandu a few days before the beginning of the Kailash package, so we had time to get a Chinese visa, but our arrival the previous Thursday evening hadn't left enough time for Krishna's brother to get our passports from the visa department. An express visa takes three days. The next morning at 9 AM, departure to Tibet was planned for the whole group, but the visa department opened an hour later, at 10 AM. We later learned of the plan: Krishna's brother Raj was supposed to go to the visa department before 10 to be the first one and to get the passports exactly at 10. The buses would leave with a big group at 9 AM on the dot, and we, with a smaller group, would catch up to the bus in a fast SUV later. We would also ride in the same SUV to the border of China. That was the plan!

Sadhu. Pashupatinath temple complex, Kathmandu, Nepal.

Budhanilkantha temple, dedicated to Vishnu.

A five-metre statue of Vishnu Kathmandu, Nepal.

By the side of the road, flames were extinguished from millions of bundles of wires, Kathmandu, Nepal.

3× Heli Grauberg, 2019

The ride to Tibet begins! Guru Purnima

KATHMANDU (Nepal) • RASUWAGADHI (Nepali and Tibet border)

16/07/19, Tuesday — As soon as Raj arrived with the passports for Maria and myself (the rest of the group had already gotten their visas in India), our journey to Kailash started shortly after 10 AM. In the SUV we were accompanied by Umesh, my guide and assistant from my previous pilgrimage, and Subir, a guide from Nepal. Also in the car were Monica and Ram, both in their thirties and living in India. Ram is a Nepali who has lived and studied in England for four years and now owns a small IT company in his new home country of India. He is a follower of Sadhguru (the founder of the Isha Foundation) and often spends time in the guru's ashram and is involved in all kinds of charitable projects. Ram very often leads the conversation to his guru and his teachings and activities. He is knowledgeable in every field, his hobby is art and he speaks very fluent English. For Ram, this was the first pilgrimage of his life to Mount Kailash.

Monica is a free spirit who is more suited to the Western world than to India. She's a bit of a tomboy. Monica works in Delhi as an engineer. On her days off, she travels alone around India, visiting the local sanctuaries and temples. She carried her *murti*, or holy figurine, with her at every meal as if he were a child - they ate and drank together, and every day she changed his dress. "When you're travelling, you can go a few days without changing," Monica said. That's how she has cared for her tiny metallic baby Krishna Laddu, the god baby, for almost 16 years. Miracles have happened to the little figurine. Once, the baby slipped through a metal detector check and sat quietly in Monica's pocket in a large sacred temple in India. Her home in India is like a holy temple itself, filled with gorgeously dressed and bejewelled statues of Hindu deities. In this life, it's Monica's third time to do the Kailash pilgrimage.

Dear reader, if you've seen some of the gruesome footage of buses and cars driving along the gorge on YouTube, that's what our trip to Nepal reminded us of. The car was constantly balancing on the edge of the muddy road, and the scenic but mind-bogglingly deep gorge yawned ominously at us.

Of course, cars and buses would occasionally meet us. Somebody had to back up and somebody had to wobble half-way on a muddy bump somewhere. Maria kept her gaze fixed on one spot to avoid getting sick, while I gazed out of the SUV window.

Our new travel companion Monica (left) and Maria, with the help of an invisible rope, pulling a car that had run off the road (photo taken on the way back, when our team of guides and Sherpas were needed for this operation).

Heli Grauberg, 2019

Our new travel companion Ram at Lake Manasarovar, chanting mantras and meditating.
Ram Gurung's private colletion, 2019

God Krishna figure at Monica's home.
Monica Sharma, 2020

Gurus

The day we were travelling happened to be the day of Guru Purnima, the day dedicated to the Teacher. A guru is a spiritual Teacher – a guide who has reached the highest level of consciousness. On this day, they are honoured and remembered. On Guru Purnima, pupils reconfirm their dedication to their Teacher and express a wish to do more spiritual practices. We talked about this important day in the car. Maria's Teacher is Ingvar Villido, whose spiritual name is Ishwarananda. I myself consider two gurus my Teachers – Yogiraj Gurunath Siddhanath from India and Ishwarananda from Estonia. From both of them I have received invaluable yoga practice consecrations and guidance for spiritual development over the years (they have different teachings and practices). Established wisdom says that a student should have only one guru, but that's my situation... And I address them both every morning, chanting the guru mantra, wishing them good health and thanking them for being there.

Ingvar Villido Ishwarananda is an Estonian Kriya yoga master, teacher and founder of the *Practical Consciousness*. His teaching style is also Estonian – crisp, simple and practical, yet technically precise. Although Ingvar has received many initiations from masters of different traditions over the years, he has recognised his true roots in the teachings of the *siddhas,* or wise men who have attained perfection, and he is also one of the extraordinary people who have completed the path of liberation described by the *siddhas*.

Ingvar Villido Ishwarananda
Siim Villido, 2020

As a *kriya* yoga *acharya,* he is qualified to teach Babaji's Kriya Yoga I, II and III- level techniques, which he himself calls the best tools for human development. He created the Practical Consciousness method, which teaches people to live without disturbing thoughts and emotions, to access the qualities of consciousness, and live in a state of flow. The basis of Ingvar's teachings is the conscious usage of the conscience, and he notes the importance of a person's own activities as the architect of one's own life and faith.

I got interested in Ingvar's (Ishwarananda) teachings thanks to my first yoga teacher, Annika, who had been studying for years at Lilleoru. After I found my way to the teachings, my life got better, and I realised the deep meaning of the wisdom "Change yourself and the world changes around you".

Yogiraj Gurunath Siddhanath is a simple, yet remarkable man. Born in Gwalior (northern), India on May 10, 1944, he is descended from the ancient royal family of Ikshavaku Rama of the Solar Dynasty. Despite his ancestry, he attained perfection and bliss at the age of 3 and chose to fulfill his calling as a yogi after completing his education. He spent his early years in the Himalayas with the great Nath Yogis; Yogiraj was blessed and empowered by the spiritual supermen of the Himalayan caves.

Today, as a Master of Kundalini Kriya Yoga, Yogiraj Gurunath has worked ceaselessly, lighting a spark in our souls and planting a seed in us to embrace, embody and support "Earth Peace Through Self Peace".

Yogiraj Gurunath Siddhanath.
Photo by Yoga Parampara

In the spirit of service, Yogiraj and his wife, Gurumata built the Siddhanath Forest Ashram in the gentle valley of Sita Mai outside the City of Pune, in India's Simhagad region. Gurumata Shivangini is a powerful Yogini in her own right. Together, they have raised two children, are proud grandparents and continue to demonstrate by example; that it is not necessary to live as a renunciate — meditating in order to achieve enlightenment — but it is more important to experience life.

Yogiraj has healed and transformed so many all over the world with his transmissions of Kundalini Shakti energy and has shared freely his own Samadhi (enlightened state) of peaceful bliss-consciousness (shortened text on the *Siddhanath Yoga Sangh* website).

When I moved to England, Ashwin Sathyamoorthy was my next yoga class instructor. He happened to have a good relationship with Rudra Shivananda, a Teacher from the USA with Indian roots, who had initiated me to Babaji's *Kriya* Yoga level III in 2008 during an intensive week-long retreat in Lilleoru (and was also the main speaker at a yoga festival in Estonia in 2014). The world is so small! The two men were united by a common guru - Yogiraj Gurunath Siddhanath.

Later, Ashwin introduced me to Gurunath himself — both on retreats and privately in his home, where the guru often stayed while teaching in London.

Every Tuesday, however, there were joint practices with the London Siddhanath Yoga Sangh group (also known as Hamsa Yoga, an association of students and teachings of Yogiraj Gurunath Siddhanath). Gatherings were mostly held at the home of our lovely Hamsa Yoga teacher and organiser Meera Venkatesan, but also at the homes of Snezhina Gulubova and Charles Suren, our dedicated instructors and organisers. After an hour of group meditation, the evening always ended with a delicious dinner and good conversation.

Our new travel companion, Ram, is dedicated to Indian yogi, writer and mystic Sadhguru Jaggi Vasudev. This man created the famous Isha Foundation, which offers different yoga courses, environmental-themed study programs and lots of other courses and charity projects. Ram says about his guru: "According to Sadhguru himself he makes people bloom to their full potential. I am just one flower in his garden and blessed to be able to serve him."

Ram wrote a poem "Guru":

Who is Guru,
what is Guru,
my body does not know, it knows only pain and pleasure,
my mind does not know, it knows only joy and suffering
my emotions don't know, they know only likes and dislikes,
my energies do not know, they only know lethargy and intensity,
only my being knows, the core of my being knows,
and that is all,
and that is all.
Shambho...

Sadhguru is a yogi and a mystic, a man whose passion spills into everything he encounters. Named one of India's 50 most influential people, Sadhguru's work has touched the lives of millions worldwide through his transformational programs. Sadhguru has a unique ability to make the ancient yogic sciences relevant to contemporary minds, acting as a bridge to the deeper dimensions of life. His approach does not ascribe to any belief system, but offers methods for self-transformation that are both proven and powerful (shortened text on the *Isha Foundation* website).

Sadhguru Jaggi Vasudev. Ram's vision about his guru. Author of the drawing Ram Gurung

Monica is a self-practitioner – she has no guru.

In the evening, at six o'clock, we arrived in a hotel near the Rasuwagadhi border point, where truck drivers and pilgrims often sleep before crossing the Nepali-Chinese border. Dinner in the cafeteria was generous and tasty, but I did not feel like eating. While conversing with Monica and Maria at the table, it turned out that the three of us had a pulsating third eye chakra, or energy centre, located in the centre of the forehead, on this particular day of Guru Purnima. Was it because it was an important day, that we were approaching the "City of the Gods", or was it something else? We couldn't find an answer to that question – it was beyond our comprehension.

There was a crowd having a big party till late at night in the hotel bar, and the AC made loud noises all night. In the morning, we realised that we didn't even have AC in our room! The noise turned out to be the mad rushing of the Karnali River outside the hotel room window. I myself had incredible trouble sleeping on that trip - two nights without sleep, the third night with 3-4 hours of sleep, then two nights without sleep again and another night with only 3-4 hours of sleep.... And it all started in Nepal. I have only had sleep issues at yoga camps and retreats (many people have this problem there), or on mornings that require waking up super early. However, I had never experienced anything like this in my life, so I was surprised that I was still functioning.

We met some Russian girls in the hotel who were also headed to Mount Kailash. Maria started a conversation and we learned that they were doing the whole hike with just the two of them plus a guide. One more Russian friend was supposed to join them, but at the last minute they decided not to give her a visa, because she had recently travelled to a country that the Chinese didn't like. Technically, there are no trips to Mount Kailash allowed with such small groups (at least from Nepal), but the Russians allegedly have good relations with the Chinese concerning that topic.

The chocolate egg problem at the Chinese border

RASUWAGADHI / KERUNG-RASUWA (Nepalese and Tibetan border) • KYIRONG (Tibet)

17/07/19, Wednesday – In the morning, with our group of 36, plus guides and Sherpas, we entered the deserted-looking border office at Rasuwagadhi, just a short walk from our hotel in Nepal the night before. However, it only looked empty; Chinese officials were waiting for us inside the spacious and sterile building. I was the first of our group to pass through the border checkpoint. None of the staff spoke any English, and they all seemed very apathetic. I took three fingerprints and then thumbprints in front of an important official, and I was automatically photographed. I nodded formally to the young man in the border booth, and with no further ado, I was officially and with no trouble on Chinese territory. But was I?

I had brought many chocolate eggs from home that were copies of bird eggs. Very nifty, true imitations. Seated on a bench on the Chinese side, waiting for the other pilgrims in the group, I noticed that the eggs had been taken out of a large bag by the staff at the border post and placed separately on one of the tables. I had brought them as snacks to boost my energy in the thin air high on Mount Kailash. It was a bit of a pity to lose those sweets, but were these eggs worth confronting the border officials? I decided they were indeed worth it! I saw our guide Umesh coming out of the border checkpoint and complained to him. Umesh promised to see what he could do. He told the Chinese guide about the problem, and he in turn went to talk to the border guards about it, with a serious look on his face. Eventually, I was called over to those in charge, who had confiscated the eggs. I showed them, by popping the treat in my mouth, that it was not really an egg, but pure chocolate. That was the end of the show; the chocolate eggs were returned to me, and when I finally left the border, the others were waiting for me.

Next, I was placed in one car with Ram, Monica, Maria and a local Chinese driver who was supposed to drive us from the border point to 2,700-metre-high Kyirong (also Gyirong) city. In the car, we really wanted to know: Was there something wrong with the driver's nerves, or was he intentionally trying to make us mad? Every five seconds, until we reached our destination, he kept changing radio stations, the other hand proudly on the wheel, speakers screaming behind our backs. Thankfully, we were soon in the hotel at Kyirong. If we exclude the flooding problem in the lobby, our accommodations were quite decent – clean sheets, nice TV, recent renovations, warm water and even a hairdryer. After the water emergency was cleaned up, the whole group enjoyed Indian food made by our boys (our kitchen staff consisting of Sherpas, guides and other helpers; from now on I will just call them the boys) and when we were full, Maria and I headed to town to look around. The only place we visited was a small Kyriong Buddhist monastery called Pakba. The city was full of deserted shops where the sellers neither greeted us nor smiled, and you could only find Chinese products, though we might have expected as much. The bland nature of the small town reminded me the old familiar Soviet times, except that there were more products in Kyirong.

We didn't walk for long, and we were back by dinnertime. This was the night they began handing out half of a Diamox tablet to prevent mountain sickness; we took it every evening until we reached Mount Kailash.

The chocolate eggs that caused such problems with the Chinese officials at the Rasuwagadhi border point.

Maria. A walk to the border point of Rasuwagadhi from the Nepalese hotel.

Pakba monastery, Kyirong, Tibet.

Road accident, Tibet

Highway and a woman with a shovel, Tibet.

Photos by Heli Grauberg, 2019

Confusion with Chinese military officials

KYIRONG • SAGA (Tibet)

18/07/19, Thursday – In the morning, the boys brought us sweet spiced *chai* in bed, and a bigger feast was planned under the skies of Tibet. As we left the hotel, a bright child's babble was coming from the lobby, but there was no one to be seen, and no one sitting at the reception desk. However, out of curiosity, I looked over to the service desk and, oh my, there was the hotel administrator and her two-year-old baby sleeping in a bed made of chairs.

Departure was in the morning at ten and we were given Chinese buses and drivers and their guide, as mandated. The roads were very good in this country; you couldn't compare the experience to the muddy roads of Nepal. Circling along the highway and arriving at an altitude of about 5,200 metres above sea level (Ram's altimeter reading), we were faced with unexpected amounts of road work, so we had to sit in the buses at the top until the workmen finally let us through.

We stopped our vehicle in a nice field about 4,800 metres above sea level and ate a hot lunch made earlier by the boys. Now the road to Saga could begin. Once we had arrived, Maria, Ram, and I put our bags in the hotel and headed out to take a look at the town. We made plans to visit the river. Unfortunately, we hadn't done our homework, so we didn't know that Saga was a true military town, where a Chinese garrison was patrolling. We walked through the city 4,640 metres above sea level and got to a place that seemed like a border point. We decided to quietly walk through it, but men in Chinese uniforms stopped us, and their gestures told us we should stay and wait. After a while, there were more officials, and we didn't understand why they didn't let us back in, although passing through this point was not allowed. Nobody spoke English, so they consulted a translation app on their phone (the same system is used in the Chinese shops). I said in English: "We are going to the river." A Chinese military man in uniform quickly entered his own Chinese text, asking: "Are you coming from Lhasa?" Hello, do they really think that the three of us came on foot from Lhasa, hundreds and hundreds of kilometres away? By this time, they had found an English-speaking official and the thing was solved amicably. We weren't allowed to go to the river, but we were allowed to go back to our hotel.

When we got back, we found a hot meal waiting for us, and Ram, the IT guy, installed a Turbo VPN app for me and Maria so we could use Facebook, Messenger, and Google while in China, since they are blocked in that country. Because we couldn't google, Turbo VPN was accessible via Bluetooth from Ram's phone. It was not unusual to get a notification from an application already in our phones: "Usage is prohibited." Then the best solution was to just uninstall it and install back again. By regularly doing so, we could sometimes get to take a glance at our Facebook or Messenger and do some googling.

Maria and Ram. Military city Saga, on our way to the river, Tibet

6x Heli Grauberg, 2019

*Lake Manasarovar, Tibet.
Our group of pilgrims who fill their water bottles and take a dip in the lake.*

Heli Grauberg, 2019

As prescribed, I jumped completely underwater three times: the first time for myself, the second in honour of my ancestors, and the third in the name of the gurus or teachers. Maria Palts, 2019

At Lake Manasarovar, waiting for the gods dance

SAGA • LAKE MANASAROVAR • LAKE RAKSHASTAL (Tibet)

19/07/19, Friday – I had suffered from insomnia for quite a while. Still the same: two nights without sleep, a few hours the third night and then again two nights without a sleep cycle. I had never taken sleeping pills, and I doubted that the high mountains were the best place to experiment, even when somebody had them on hand.

Breakfast was rice porridge and cereal. It was a nice change from our everyday Indian breakfast. I love Indian cuisine very much, but those spicy tastes and smells are a bit too much in the morning. At 8 AM, we departed for our excursion to the sacred Lake Manasarovar. Almost everyone was now taking Diamox tablets, so we needed to go to the toilet frequently. We always had to beg the Chinese bus driver in white gloves to stop along the roadside, but fortunately, he was a very kind man and always stopped. At Lake Manasarovar, we were greeted by a big gate with an official guard point where they offer transport to the lake. We changed buses and made a circle around the freshwater Lake Manasarovar, located 4,590 metres high. According to Hindu beliefs, immersing yourself in the lake and drinking it's waters, supposed to free you of your sins. We learned from Monica, who had already done this trip in the previous two years, that pilgrims are not allowed to go in the water anymore. She shared with us a video on her phone showing a bucket of Manasarovar water being poured over her at a specific location. There were no such restrictions during my 2016 pilgrimage, but now there were new laws.

Somehow, we were let out of the bus at a designated spot and given 20 minutes of free time. We had a blissful chance to dip ourselves in the water and be freed of our sins. Lots of group members didn't take the opportunity, but sat on the shore, dressed in warm puffy orange jackets. I quickly changed into my summer dress and filled the bottles with Manasarovar sacred water full of the sun, moon, rainbow, and gods dance, to take this home with me. I put the bottle on the shore and went to the water up to my chest. As planned, I jumped completely under the water three times: the first dip for myself, the second for my ancestors and the third for the gurus, or teachers (this way you can dip even 108 times!). And then I quickly jumped into my towel, threw my dry clothes on and away our bus went.

We also drove by Devil's Lake, also called Rakshastal, approximately 3.7 kilometres from Lake Manasarovar. There was a mighty wind near the lake and in the water, but by Lake Manasarovar one could enjoy complete peace and quiet.

Pilgrims' accommodations are located around Lake Manasarovar. I daresay that the accommodations by the sacred water were the most ascetic of the whole trip. In addition to the aforementioned sheets used by several visitors, we had to make peace with a toilet surrounded by faeces (literally surrounded!) that was about 30 steps away from our room. Luckily, I had my own pillowcase with me, and we slept in outerwear anyway. We all slept together again – Maria, Ram, Monica, and I – and fortunately, no group members were added to the two spare beds in our room.

In the evening, our four-person group visited the Chiu Gompa monastery on the hill. Because of the continuously ascending height, we had to stop to catch our breath. We reached the destination at eight in the evening and the *gompa's* doors were closed by then. All we could do was gaze it from the outside and admire the incredible view of Lake Manasarovar below. By dinnertime, we were back in our rooms and got our nightly Diamox tablet from the guides.

There was nothing left of my appetite, so I decided to pass on late dinner, but I was not allowed to go to sleep without eating – the boys brought me some food with aromatic *chai* to my bedside: "Eat at least a little!" It was embarrassing; they had taken the trouble to do it and I was being a prim. So, I took a few small bites of the *chapata* bread with *dahl* and a cup of hot tea. At eleven at night we bunked down, dressed in jackets and long pants, and set an alarm for two at night because we were extremely eager to see the gods dance.

When we arrived at the lake in the pitch-black starry night, some pilgrims were already waiting for a miracle. Soon enough, clouds gathered in the sky and the stars disappeared. But the Moon was still showing its royal beauty and shone its charm on the sacred lake. We were on the shores of Lake Manasarovar from half past two till four o'clock in the morning. And on this Kailash pilgrimage, I was not fortunate enough to experience the magical moment. There was nothing I could do to get back to sleep, and while my roommates were getting some shuteye for a few more hours, I admired the colourful ceiling of the guesthouse, sleepless, listening to my roommates' snores.

As morning approached, I was looking for my Lake Manasarovar bottles, and – what happened? Maria had mistaken one plastic bottle for regular water and drank it all. She was one of those who hadn't taken any water to bring back home, because she doubted its drinkability. I guess she had to get her holy water dosage accidentally. When she realised what had happened, she was suddenly beset with stomach problems. Placebo or not, who knows?

Ram, Monica and Maria.
Chiu Gompa on the hill by Lake Manasarovar, Tibet.

Maria at the starting point of the Mount Kailash pilgrimage.

*Monica, Maria and Ram.
Guesthouse by lake.*

*Guides and Sherpas
handing out food under
the windows of our
Lake Manasarovar
guesthouse, Tibet.*

4x Heli Grauberg, 2019

One of the trip's highlights – through difficulties to blessings

LAKE MANASAROVAR • DARCHEN (Tibet)

20/07/19, Saturday — Our enthusiastic kitchen team had set a tea table under our window early in the morning. Our whole group went to Lake Manasarovar after breakfast. Krishna had previously arranged for a *pujari*, or Hindu priest, for the group, who would hold a *havan* (Hindu traditional fire ceremony) by the lake. The fire was lit and sacred syllables, or mantras, were sung around it. Sacrifices (rice and fruits) were made and secret wishes were whispered. Monica had her own *puja* trinkets with her – incense, a bell and a candle, so Maria and I did our own ceremony away from the larger group. Monica called on different gods, chanting mantras, inviting gods to come down to Earth and bless us. She says that in her past life she was a *pujari,* or Hindu temple priest. Maybe she's right about her past life, and that's why she's so good with these rituals.

By the beautiful, shimmering morning lake, a few people wanted to dip themselves in the holy waters of Manasarovar once more. Of course, they didn't succeed, because as if on cue, a female guard in Tibetan clothes arrived, a big official tag hanging around her neck, waving her arms angrily, ordering them to cease and desist.

Guide Umesh's morning greeting in the Lake Manasarovar, Tibet.

Umesh's private collection

Monica, Maria and Heli puja at Lake Manasarovar, Tibet.
   Umesh Giri, 2019

Our group's havan by Lake Manasarovar.
   Heli Grauberg, 2019

Around one in the afternoon we packed our bags and got on a bus, headed to Darchen. This is a village 4,575 metres above sea level and a starting point for pilgrims. A rather nice guesthouse was waiting for us upon arrival to Darchen. We got an apartment-type accommodation, which suited our group perfectly – Maria with me in a room for two, Ram and Monica in single rooms. The toilet was shared by the four of us. We even had warm water, but the shower head happened to be broken, so there was not much talk about washing in that village.

Krishna had previously talked to our Tibetan guide about Ashtapad (see Ashtapad, chapter "Kailash *inner kora*, or inner circle") to organise entrance permits for Maria, Monica and me.

This is just one small part of the *inner kora*. Many saints supposedly meditate in the caves, from which there is a magnificent view of the southern side of nearby Mount Kailash, where a spine-like line runs through the middle of the mountain. Unfortunately, the guide didn't show any interest in catering to our wishes and simply said: "The weather is not that clear at all and you'll find no beautiful view there." Monica said: "We don't care, we're not going for the view!" Hours passed, and we waited and waited and waited. We knew it was the only time of the trip when we would have this kind of free time near Darchen to visit the Ashtapad. After an SMS to the owner of the Nepali travel agency, things seemed to be moving along, and the guide was already telling us that our permits were being processed.

The next morning was the beginning of the pilgrimage, which demanded some strength, but that didn't interest us – we wanted to get as much as we could out of the trip and were ready for an evening, even for a night-time hike. We sat in our hotel room for hours and waited for news about the Ashtapad permits. We got completely fed up with this situation by six in the evening and went to shop in the Darchen village. We had to buy an oxygen tank and a camping stick for the upcoming pilgrimage – you never know what you might need. While wandering around the booths and shops, we saw Umesh, who called to us: "The car has arrived, you can go to Ashtapad!" We ran to our hotel through the rain as fast as we could, grabbed our bags and paid a decent sum to Tibetan guide for this trip and for the permits. The time was already half past seven, but if we're going, let's go! We paid the money without seeing the permit and didn't even know where we were being taken, but Monica, Maria and I still got in the car with this monolingual driver and were headed to Ashtapad, to the best of our knowledge.

After an approximately 20-minute ride, the man stopped the car and let us leave the car. He gestured with his hands; we understood that he was suggesting that we take photos of the mountains in the background. He put some creek water into a bottle and brought it to us three, looking happy. We did take some photos and got back into the vehicle to continue to Ashtapad. But to our surprise, the driver turned around and started to take us back to Darchen. This was it? Monica started yelling, gesturing to the monolingual driver, yelling "What about Ashtapad? And actually, we would like to call our Tibetan guide right away!" The driver kept repeating to our Ashtapad chant: "Police, police!"

It was obvious that the driver was very nervous about all this and our new Indian friend didn't exactly hold back. We finally drove to an area that had reception and Monica got a chance to call our Tibetan guide. The main message was: "Is this what we paid for? This 20-minute drive?!" The call was cut off and Monica asked the driver for the guide's number. He refused. Luckily, the guide called us right back. While the phone was still in Monica's hands, she quickly wrote down the number on her hand while the driver tried to grab the phone back. The situation in the car was full of tension. I don't know what Monica and the guide finally talked about, but the vehicle turned around and we headed in a completely different direction until we reached a small house (we still don't have accurate info about the exact name) and a white ribbon prohibiting passage to Ashtapad, Kailash and Mount Nandi.

We drove to where few people set foot, and it was one of the top moments of our pilgrimage. We visited a place where the travellers of the *inner kora* usually end (or begin, as the case may be) their pilgrimage. When we arrived, creamy white clouds started to fade around the mountain. And what an amazing view on the south side of Kailash – where Meru Danda runs through the middle of the mountain like a spine – and beautiful Nandi. Monica picked her things out of her bag again and held a little ceremony. The clouds in the background became more and more sparse and an incredible view opened up of Mounts Nandi and Kailash.

Sitting on the ground and looking at the holy mountain, it was as if I saw small silver glints of light flashing. As if they were sparks from somebody's eyes. I don't know what it was. In this sacred place, we three could be a part of blessings, so our tears kept falling uncontrollably, but there were no emotions...

The driver softened when he saw three women in tears – he lit our candle for the *puja* ritual with his lighter and brought his tissue box from the car so we could dry our tears. Regardless of what happened to our Ashtapad permits, or what the guide organised or what the driver understood, 120 USD wasn't much to pay for this kind of blessing, or *darshan,* and an amazing view; it was a once-in-a-lifetime experience. There's no chance we could have ended up in this place by chance. Maybe one day we will reach Ashtapad. We silently drove back, were very happy and Monica gave a small chocolate to the driver as a thanks.

Top moments of the trip. Blessings on the south sides of Mountains Nandi and Kailash. Monica standing next to the white ribbon prohibiting passage to Ashtapad.

Top moments of the trip. Blessings on the south sides of Mountains Nandi and Kailash.
2x Heli Grauberg, 2019

Two adventures in one day – 1st day of *kora* and a hike to Charan Sparsh

DARCHEN • DIRAPUK (Tibet)

21/07/19, Sunday – Finally, the pilgrimage circle around Mount Kailash could begin. Everything that had come before – visas, permits to enter the mountain, being in Kathmandu, the long bus ride, acclimatisation, Diamox tablets – they were just the leadup to the three important days ahead. Everything looked promising – the weather was beautiful, and the mood was great. Our backpacks were full of packed foods for the day; they contained a *samosa,* or fried pocket filled with vegetables, chocolate, a small juice, half an apple packed into foil and cookies. It was extremely comfortable having the kitchen team with the group all the time, absolutely no worrying about the food.

Maria and I decided not to use the porter service and carried the three days' supplies ourselves in a backpack, plus the water supply for one day and an oxygen tank. Taking a packager was rather expensive, and it is not always easy to coordinate with the helpers, because they may well run behind or in front with the water bottles, food, toilet paper and other necessities. A porter or horse must be paid for on the first day of *kora,* paying all pilgrimage days in advance. If you wish to hire a helper later, it's said to be a rather impossible try – you must decide at the beginning of the *kora.*

First day of kora, Tibet.
Heli Grauberg, 2019

Meeting with a Tibetan woman.

First day of kora, Tibet. Second pilgrimage with guide Umesh.

2x Ram Gurung, 2019

The weather was perfect for a walk around Mount Kailash. Many pilgrims (mostly from India) had rented horses and enjoyed amazing mountain views from a bit higher up. Maria and I stopped to sit on the rocks a few times.

We ate what had been packed for us and used the outdoor toilets on the pilgrimage road. You could buy noodle soup, *chai*, and other snacks from the tent-cafeteria; there were not many choices, of course. We kept walking and walking, sometimes taking photos and drinking water, chanting mantras. While circling the mountain, I often forgot where I was and why I had come here. When I remembered, I tried to get all those small pointless thoughts out of my head and dedicated myself to repeating the mantra of Lord Shiva…

On the first day of *kora*, you just walk by the dusty camp road. The thin air makes the walk a lot slower and more difficult than a casual walk in the park at home.

One woman in our group finished eating her sweets from a big, colourful plastic bag and then just threw it on the ground over her shoulder. Maria ran up to the middle-aged Indian woman and asked if she had lost something. The woman glanced at her bag, shrugged her shoulders and quietly paced on, eating her sweets. I still feel guilty for not running back and picking up that bag with Maria.

So, there we were at our destination, Dirapuk (5,080 metres above sea level), where pilgrims usually arrive at the end of the day's hike. We were greeted by a new and cleaner guesthouse, with some rooms which had an amazing view of the snowy Mount Kailash. If the toilets had been inside, it would have been an ultra-luxurious experience in the expanses of Tibet. Again, Maria and I managed to get one room with Monica and Ram and got to our beds immediately.

Yay! The first day of *kora* was done! Actually, we had planned our next hike to Charan Sparsh, foot of Kailash, on the same evening. Touching this slope was supposed to be comparable with touching Shiva's feet. We didn't manage to lie down, though, since Umesh came to our room straightaway and told us we could head out to Charan Sparsh. We had agreed on the hike with Umesh before, but everyone who has the will and the strength can walk there on their own. At the same time, you must consider that the next, second day of *kora* is the hardest.

Walking at a relaxed pace took Ram, Umesh and me about one-and-a-half hours. During this time, we managed to climb some very slippery rocks and jump over some smaller creeks. Maria and Monica took things more easily and followed us slowly.

Quite a lot of pilgrims had taken the road to Charan Sparsh that day – some led prayer ceremonies, some were just in the moment and some captured a lot of photos. Monica organised a small vesper at the foot and I created a small snowman made by an Estonian.

The foot is visually very close to Mount Kailash, but for safety purposes, you can't go ahead without a guide helper – it might not even be allowed.

I noticed that our guide, Umesh, gathered all the trash pilgrims had left at the foot of the mountain in a plastic bag – for example, trash and other smaller things that were left after holding ceremonies – and brought it with him to the guesthouse to throw away.

When we got back to the hotel, we got word that there was a strike somewhere in the Kailash region and nobody could be around the mountain on the 23th of July. Anyone who wished to do the *kora* would have to complete the kilometres of the second and third day in one day. We searched for information about this strike from different sources but nobody had heard about it. Was our group wanted back quickly, hoping we would not go and do two days in one? Or was it a strike? We never found out. Usually, after the second day of *kora*, you go to Zutulpuk, spend the night, and regain strength to begin the third and last day of *kora* the next morning. Now we would be doing all the path in one day.

We always had unlimited water, but that day something had happened to the group's drinking water, and the kitchen team could only offer water boiled on the spot. So, I filled my bottles with hot water and hoped I had enough supplies for the two-in-one pilgrimage.

2nd and 3rd day of *kora* – God Shiva, if you want, take me!

DIRAPUK • ZUTULPUK • DARCHEN (Tibet)

"God Shiva, if you want, take me!" Lord Shiva at Ramna Kali Temple & Anandamayi Ma Ashram, Dhaka Bangladesh. Heli Grauberg, 2022

22/07/19, Monday – Wakeup was at four in the morning because two of the *kora* days were back-to-back. But I didn't need an alarm because I had stared at the ceiling all night, trying to sleep. The same old pattern – still the same unbelievable insomnia: two days without sleep, the third night 3-4 hours and then again two nights without sleep, and another night of 3-4 hours of sleep. Why did my second sleepless night have to fall on the hardest day when I had to cross the highest point – Dolma La Pass, 5,630 meters above sea level – and continue with a third day of *kora* in terrible weather?

Two demanding hikes and a previous sleepless night didn't exactly help me fall asleep. In the early morning, I was half crazy because of the insomnia, while I was tottering to the outside toilet during a terrible downpour. I was tired and spent, thinking about quitting the pilgrimage — *am I really capable of doing this hike after two sleepless nights? In pitch black and a big downpour, beginning my journey, passing two days of kora in one day?* I was not sure if the helicopters would be able to get to me in the snow, at the highest point of the hike, should I need help.

When I got back to our room, short of breath, Maria told me she wouldn't take the risk; she would join the other members of the group going back to the Darchen village. She couldn't assess her abilities and didn't want to be a burden on Monica, Ram, Umesh, and me, if her strength should give out. "I have got enough as it is from this pilgrimage! Visiting Lake Manasarovar and the monastery on the same hill, the foot of Mount Kailash — Charan Sparsh — and the special blessings on the south side of Mountains Nandi and Kailash and, of course, the successful first day of *kora*" she said. Now I got scared... *Is it really the right decision to go on this road, exhausted as I am? I can't even carry my backpack in this state.* I told Umesh sleepily: "I need a porter." I knew it was not possible to order this service halfway through the trip, and Umesh was wearing his and Monica's backpacks from the first day already. But Umesh suggested sending my stuff back to Darchen with Maria and other pilgrims of our group. What else do I need for one day in my bag besides an oxygen tank, drinking water, food, and camera? This solution gave me an incredible burst of energy and of course, I decided to go on the path, to continue my pilgrimage. Those who chose to go back to Darchen were picked up by local emergency vehicles, and every pilgrim had to pay 500 Chinese yuan for that.

I gave Maria all my stuff that was supposed to go back to Darchen. I pulled on a thin windbreaker with no lining over an Indian-style linen dress and stepped outside to finish my pilgrimage. It was raining cats and dogs and it was pitch black outside. As I stepped out of the hotel, I looked at Shiva's home, holy Mount Kailash, through pouring rain, tears in my eyes, and said in my mind: "God Shiva, if you want, take me!"

Ram and Monica were already waiting for me outside. I stood next to them, yarn socks in my hiking boots, bare hands, wearing a thin jacket with no lining and a raincoat. I noticed only that I had no gloves. Ram gave me a break and went to get the gloves himself. Maria couldn't find them among my stuff and gave me her gloves. When Ram arrived with them, the early crispiness and humidity had gotten into my bones, and I discovered myself shivering in a thin jacket, without even a warm hoodie to put on underneath it. I guess this kind of equipment was not the best to take on a long hike through rain and snow. I kept my companions waiting once more and ran upstairs to get my other jacket. Seeing me tottering to the room, Maria sat me down on the bed and said: "Heli, are you absolutely sure you are going?!" Running up the stairs wasn't a good idea in this kind of air, because it really stole the last breath of a sleep-deprived person. Hmmm… had someone up there made this pilgrimage so hard for me through this insomnia? I fear neither snow nor rain, nor a long hike. It is only the high mountains– I have great respect for and that's not to be joked about. Wouldn't the pilgrimage be strength consuming as it is, even without the insomnia? The Mount Kailash tour three years ago had been a pleasure, with beautiful sunny weather, a normal sleep cycle, a personal guide and a hike spread over four days (with an extra day taken for Charan Sparsh).

Six months earlier, I had bought myself a very important item – sunscreen with a high SPF factor. Based on my kora experience in early 2016, I really needed it, because my face had gotten sunburned and blistered. This important fact didn't occur to me early in the morning, and the tube of cream travelled safely with Maria to the village of Darchen instead. Yes, I had planned this trip to Tibet six months in advance, but I still set off unprepared.

The time was almost six o'clock when we could finally begin the second and third day of *kora* with Ram and Monica. We tried to find the right road with flashlights, and suddenly my small, and of course very cheap (but also brand new) flashlight landed in a puddle of water and broke into pieces. With the help of Monica's light, we found the parts and put the thing together again so we could move on. The result of this mess was that my thin woollen gloves borrowed from Maria got wet straightaway. We just couldn't find the right road. Finally, we saw a figure in the darkness, and Ram called: "*Kora, kora?*", and a Tibetan man showed us the right way. Soon enough, Ram was completely gone, but thankfully we found him soon; he had just gone out to find the path alone.

The path we chose with the help of the Tibetan was a shortcut and was the quickest way up. It was quite difficult in the beginning to get up the path beside the steep stone mountain. To get up the hill from the slippery stones, one had to exert one more effort, but we felt we couldn't. Suddenly, two dark eyes looked at us in the darkness above and they extended a helping hand. It was probably the same man who had shown us the road before. After some time, Umesh joined us. The four of us slowly marched through the downpour to Dolma La Pass; we were sitting on the slippery stones after every 10 steps, or just standing to catch a breath. The thin air made itself known now. The rain ended shortly thereafter, and higher grounds greeted us with a beautiful whitish-blue carpet of snow and bright morning sun rays shining over the hilltops. The view was like some commercial photograph of an Austrian ski centre. What peace flowed over me up there, and how breathtakingly beautiful it all was. This time was different, as if I had never been to Dolma La Pass before. A completely new experience.

This year the overall atmosphere around the mountain and the weather were completely different from how they had been three years ago on the second day of *kora*—there were no big Indian pilgrim groups on the road, only local Tibetans with their families. Indian pilgrims probably missed the holy pilgrimage because of the alleged strike and bad weather. Tibetans on the road though, old and young, were moving incredibly fast and passed us soon enough. We didn't have to feel embarrassed because the Tibetans can do this thanks to their famous high-altitude gene. They had taken children from various age groups with them. Some were so little that their feet didn't carry them yet. They were attached in packs on their parents' backs. Older children marched proudly next to their parents and relatives.

Our friend Ram, who encouraged Monica and me in the morning, trying to boost our spirits, got tired too, and needed to rest on the way up after every few steps. Ram even dreamt about a bed! Earlier, he had told us that he was counting on his Nepali genes to support him up high in the thin Himalayan air.

Snowy and wet stones under our feet were at times dangerously slippery. And how my feet squelched all the way in wet hiking boots! Thanks to that, I lost one toenail later on, and without any protective cream, my face got rough treatment under the high mountain sun.

Finally, we reached the culmination, the highest point of the Mount Kailash pilgrimage, Dolma La Pass, also known as the place of symbolic rebirth, 5,630 metres above sea level. Anyone can leave something of theirs behind there, something symbolic from the past. For example, a tuft of hair, a hat, a piece of clothing, etc. I had nothing superfluous with me, because all my stuff had been driven to the Darchen village in an ambulance car. But I really wanted to leave something behind, and I got my wish. I still had some of the chocolate eggs with me that had been confiscated on the Chinese border and later returned. So, I left one there. At least compostable!

Deep in the valley, the surreal emerald Gauri Kund—the lake where the god Shiva's wife Parvati washed herself and gave birth to the deity Ganesha—was glistening in the sun's rays, surrounded by white snow. Going down to the lake in such weather would have been dangerous even for our guide Umesh, so I didn't drink the nectar of this lake on this trip, nor did I bring it home.

The descent to Dolma La Pass is rather steep and was especially demanding because the stones were slippery from the rain and snow. I wouldn't have made it this time without a hiking stick. Water kept flowing into my boots from my calves, and it was hard to walk around in those. But the Tibetan smiles and greetings— *"Tashi Delek!"* —improved my mood. One small boy even gave me his hand when I had to jump from one stone to another. And I got a piece of candy! And I, in my morning confusion, had forgotten all the stickers, cars, felt-tips and other treasures that I had brought with me from home; I'd left them in a plastic bag on its way back to Darchen with Maria.

During the ascent, everything got much easier—there was enough air to breathe again, and it became an easy path to walk. In the distance we could see a field filled with Tibetan horses and yaks eating grass.

Finally, we reached Zutulpuk. According to the initial plan, we were supposed to rest in the guesthouse, eat dinner and sleep for a night. But this luxury was to be only a dream this time. In Zutulpuk, we sat on the roadside, gathered some strength, and went on, to the end of the *kora*, Darchen. An Indian woman Daya joined our group; she had also gathered her courage to start the second and third days of her pilgrimage with her mother and one other guide. Her mother had turned back straightaway, and their guide passed the woman on to our group of four. Only four people joined this pilgrimage of 36 that day.

It was six-thirty in the evening when we started moving towards Darchen from Zutulpuk. We needed to walk rather fast, because we definitely had to reach the destination by the end of the day. At some point, it was raining cats and dogs, but that was good; it made us walk faster. Fortunately, the third day's path is very easy and short—"like a walk in the park". Our heavy wet boots weren't as uncomfortable, because the road was straight and simple. Tibetans kept passing us, and Bon believers, doing the *kora* counterclockwise, met us with the same fast pace. For locals, it's normal to do several *kora* days in one day, maybe even all three. When we got the signal, Umesh contacted our Chinese helpers so they could send transportation to us at the end of the path. We didn't want to walk the 3.5 more kilometres to Darchen village that the local Tibetans, unlike Indian and Western pilgrims, pass on foot. Unfortunately, we found out that no car or bus would be sent to meet us. It was not our fault that only four people of 36 went to make the *kora*. We were surprised. After a few phone calls between Umesh and the Chinese helpers, everything had been worked out, and there was a travel bus waiting for us at the end of the path.

After a 14-hour hike, we finally found ourselves in the Darchen village hotel. They had been expecting us. Maria had turned on the electric heaters in all three beds and as soon as I got to the room, she helped me get out of my soaking wet boots. The boys brought us sweet hot chai, which tasted especially good after this trip. Maria told me about her morning adventures in the ambulance car that had taken her back to Darchen. It could officially accommodate only six passengers, but they made it seven. When he saw a police car coming, the driver ordered them to lay down, so one of the group members threw herself on the floor of the car and the others covered her with a jacket.

At dinner, one of our guides came to me and asked if I hike in the mountains in my everyday life, to which I answered: "Oh no, this is my third biggest hike, after the last Kailash circle and climbing to Guadeloupe volcano mountain." I felt the gazes of the Indian pilgrimage group members on us. Maybe some felt sorry that they hadn't travelled the road with us… Or whatever they thought… One Hindu woman came to me, touched me on the shoulder and slightly bowed in front of me, hands in the prayer position. I bowed back and felt embarrassed…

Photos: Combined 2nd and 3rd days of kora.

Early morning, Tibet.

Tibetan family. Early morning, Tibet.

Monica. Early morning, Tibet.

Early morning, Tibet.

Combined 2nd and 3rd days of kora, Tibet.

Some were so small, their feet didn't carry them yet, so they were tied to backs, Tibet.

Morning near Dolma La Pass, Tibet.

Emerald green Gauri Kund, Tibet.

Combined 2nd and 3rd day of kora.
    We got down and it was green again. Tibetans making full-prostration, Tibet.
            Photos by Heli Grauberg, 2019

Sleep is back!

DARCHEN • SAGA (Tibet)

23/07/19, Tuesday – Finally, that night, I slept, and after that, I was able to sleep again. I don't know if the last day's 14-hour hike helped, when I passed the tests sent from the higher forces, or if it was just that it was the end of the pilgrimage.

In the morning, Monica told us about her last Kailash kora experience where the weather was so bad that pilgrims of her group were not even allowed on the track by the organisers. Monica, of course, didn't accept it and made a big fuss. It ended with her and an American girl writing up a statement that declared that they accepted all the risks and liabilities of this pilgrimage, so those two and a guide went ahead. And the weather was even better than we have now in 2019!

Early in the morning we had some hot *chai* in the hotel lobby and the departure could begin, starting at 6:00 AM heading towards the military town Saga.

Our group consisted of Hindus only, and most of them lived in India (Ram had Nepali roots, but lived in India). Some of the people in the group were slightly older people for whom the two-in-one hike might really be a bit too much. Indian pilgrims are often a bit older (but then again, because of the high-altitude conditions, young and fit individuals don't necessarily make it very far either!). Sometimes they just plan a hike to Lake Manasarovar, hoping to get at least a glimpse of the holy mountain and receive some blessings. Many Hindus come from India every year to do the pilgrimage on the hills of Kailash. Groups often consist of 50-60 people. According to statistics, only a small percentage of pilgrims are thought to complete the full *outer kora*.

Renting a horse is not cheap, but it does offer those with less strength the ability to travel. But even a horse doesn't necessarily help in bad weather.

Our Tibetan guide told us that very few permits are given out to enter the region of the inner circle (*inner kora*). "Very good physical form and decent hiking clothes and shoes are a must," a Tibetan guide warned us.

Ram discovered on the bus on our way to Saga that he had forgotten his wallet on the bed in the Darchen hotel. Fortunately, they reacted quickly over the phone and promised to transport this valuable item to Kathmandu through several people.

After a long bus ride, we finally arrived in Saga at three in the afternoon—the military town where Chinese soldiers had cross-examined us near the guard post last time and then sent us back the way we came. The hotel couldn't offer us a room for four, so they gave us a three-person room with one additional mattress so all the friends—Ram, Monica, Maria and I—could share a joint room. The hotel was comfortable and clean and warm water ran out of the shower. There were some signs that somebody had already slept on the sheets, but it was okay. There was a queue to shower. The beds had electrical heating that we didn't have the courage to leave on at night, but it was warm enough without them. I loaded Turbo VPN onto my phone again, went to Facebook and uploaded the first photos of our Mount Kailash pilgrimage for my friends to see. We were too tired that evening to go anywhere, so we ate our dinners and went to rest in our room. I slept well again. I suppose my insomnia had been passed on to Monica, because she had had problems sleeping the previous two nights.

Sometimes a pilgrimage is planned just to Lake Manasarovar to receive blessings by gazing at it…

Monica performing a ritual at Manasarovar Lake, Tibet. Heli Grauberg, 2019

Part of our group in the group picture, Tibet.

The trip comes to an end

SAGA • KYIRONG (Tibet)

24/07/19, Wednesday – After breakfast, we headed from the military town Saga to Kyirong.

We stopped by River Brahmaputra, which flows through Tibet, India and Bangladesh, to take a group photo. I was lucky to make this trip with my friend and to find two new travel companions to do things with during the hikes. It would have been tiresome to be alone in a big pilgrimage group full of strangers.

As the *kora* was over, I was extremely hungry. I had lost a few kilos there and wasn't planning on putting them back on. But still… Maria and I were already quietly dreaming of the spinach and cheese dish *saag paneer* and creamy cakes…

We reached Kyirong by lunchtime. The hotel, with its big TV that we didn't turn on once, was the same as it had been the last time. We took a room for two and a mattress for Monica and finally let Ram spend a night on his own in the other room. He dutifully did his yoga meditation practice every morning and chanted mantras, undisturbed by the presence of the three of us. Thanks to his previous ashram experiences, he was not disturbed by living in close quarters, nor by sharing a room with us. Now Ram could peacefully practices. I am a regular practitioner in my everyday life, but I often skip yoga practices during travels.

We ate in the hotel lobby, and I walked to a local temple with Maria and Monica to meditate a bit. After meditating in the front room of the sanctuary, we acknowledged that this small Chinese-Nepali border town was terribly boring to walk around and was probably rather depressing to live in. Almost all the shops were dimly lit and empty of customers; the sellers, sitting on their phones behind the counter, just looked through us. In a few cafeterias, some tables were occupied with locals enjoying their food. When we showed interest in something while shopping, the sellers picked up their phones and translated the foreign conversation into Chinese with the help of a translation app. A sad town without much character. Thankfully, they had a Buddhist temple, which was the only thing worth seeing. It proved to be an oasis during our short visit.

I was in for a nice surprise that evening – the boys had prepared an amazing, luxurious dinner for the whole group. This was the last dinner they would prepare on this pilgrimage around Mount Kailash.

At that moment, I was so happy that we had resisted the temptation to choose some diner out of mere curiosity about Chinese and Tibetan dishes. The kitchen team had put in a huge effort and the choice of Indian foods that evening was vast, not to mention beautifully presented. I experienced great sadness during this dinner – we were nearing the end of our trip.

Our last dinner by the kitchen team, Kyirong, Tibet.

Our Sherpas and guides in front of the Saga hotel, Tibet.

Heli Grauberg, 2019

Balancing the bus on the edge of a gorge back to Kathmandu

•KYIRONG *(Tibet)*
•RASUWAGADHI / KERUNG-RASUWA *(Nepali-Chinese border)*
•KATHMANDU *(Nepal)*

25/07/19, Thursday – Our last breakfast made by the boys was served at 07.30, and at 9.30 AM we headed from Kyirong to our familiar Nepali-Chinese Rasuwagadh border point. There was drama at the border – Monica's 12 litres of holy Lake Manasarovar water did not reach the destination with us. Yes, you read that right – 12 litres of holy water. Tears flowed and things were being cleared. The reason for the loss of the canisters was discovered and a truck with water was sent to us.

We reached the Nepalese border and the buses and drivers that had transported us in China were left behind. We got our travel agencies' buses back again, but unfortunately not the SUV. Nepali highways are very dangerous, but the scenery is amazing. We had to go through the same teetering balancing act on the gorge, but this time it was even scarier, because we were in a big bus, not a smaller SUV. The bus driver kept manoeuvring back and forth, over and over. We would occasionally pass some car or bus stuck in the mud, and our guides and Sherpas went to help them out. For hours, our lives were in the hands of a stranger, this Nepali bus driver. The big bus kept shaking and made me want to pee, despite the fact that Diamox wasn't causing this problem anymore.

We made a pit stop in a local restaurant. Lunch was included in the travel package – the boys had finished their hard work and could peacefully enjoy their meal with us now.

We arrived at Kathmandu, to our nice and clean Arts Hotel, where our large travel bags were already waiting for us. We got new rooms. This time, the hotel's bathroom was bigger than last time, and the sheets were freshly starched and pearly white; you could go to sleep naked under those sheets. All the travel agencies' representatives, Krishna in front, had come to greet the group from the pilgrimage and to have dinner with us.

The next morning, our Kailash pilgrimage package ended. There were two options – pay for the same room or move to different accommodations of our own choosing. We stayed one more night in Arts and decided to move on to the Kathmandu Guest House.

If ever again...

KATHMANDU (Nepal)

26/07/19, Friday – Is this the end of my Kailash story? Will I ever cross the threshold of the City of God? The still unseen dance of the gods on the shining light blue surface of Lake Manasarovar, unwalked paths of the inner circle... I haven't hugged the mountain itself, nor have I begun a pilgrimage straight from the capital of Tibet, Lhasa. I put the decision of my new trip kindly into Shiva's hands. What else can I do?

Maria and I did the last of our shopping, walked under the empty window of the goddess Kumari as we had done at the beginning of the trip, drank a glass of red wine in the New Orleans Café and went back to the hotel. Maria got a headache from that glass of wine and went to bed, but I went out and visited a Thamel roof terrace café.

Visiting Swayambhunath

KATHMANDU (Nepal)

27/07/19, Saturday – Maria, Monica, Ram and I took a local taxi for just the four of us in the morning and headed out on our last joint adventure – one of the important Buddhist centres of Tibet in Nepal, Swayambhunath. A sanctuary called the Temple of Apes rises above the capital, Kathmandu, and is in an energetically very special place, where people's prayers and wishes are allegedly enhanced. To get to a stupa with Buddha's eyes and other temples, you shall walk 365 steps. Catching our breath in the heat of July, once we arrived at the top, we were sweaty and tired. What a beautiful panoramic view of the city in the morning mist! Naughty apes rushed across the stupa's edges, temples, and statues. The monotonous Om Mani Padme Hum mantra could be heard sounding from a loudspeaker somewhere, and wishes were heard all over the old sanctuaries, enhanced by Swayambhunath.

A monkey sitting in the temple complex of Swayambhunath, Kathmandu, Nepal. Heli Grauberg, 2019

In the afternoon, both Monica and Ram flew to India on different flights and Maria and I moved to the Kathmandu Guest House, a few hundred metres from the Arts Hotel.

We agreed on dinner in a traditional Nepali restaurant. Local Nepali girls danced in traditional clothes, and the food and drinks were very good. Krishna had just gotten word of the death of two local Sherpas on the terrible highways that cling to the rims of Nepali gorges. We had passed that spot just a few days earlier. This sad news touched us deeply. One of topics at the dinner table was the group going on the Kailash Pilgrimage on the 5th of August – a group of 250 Nepalese and Indian people who followed the teachings of a Nepali guru. This holy man with his companions had chosen Krishna's agency among all the travel agencies. Krishna had never transported such a big group to Mount Kailash, and now he had to include almost the whole team and do a lot of work organising. Krishna was joking with me: "If you want, join!" This challenge haunted me; playing with the thought of going on a new *kora* accompanied me until falling asleep.

Really, back to Mount Kailash with a Nepali Baba?!

KATHMANDU (Nepal)

28/07/19, Sunday – I woke up with the same thoughts on my mind. Will I do another *kora* after the previous Mount Kailash circle? Physically, I was already in Nepal, travel things in my bag, valid travel insurance, no need for new plane tickets and no urgent duties waiting at home. After this circle I would have passed three *koras* already, what a cleansing and benefit (hopefully!) to my karma. Also, an adventure full of new and interesting blessings – pilgrimage with a Nepali guru, Mahayogi Siddhababa Shribaishnav Krishandasji Maharaj.

Surrounded by doctors, journalists and the faithful, the same Nepali holy man reached the state of *samadhi* for eight days in 2016 at Naranarayan Baba Ashram in Ramghat of Pokhara. This is a state of superior consciousness, when a person manages themselves completely on whole levels. Body and senses are resting as if sleeping, but the mind and spirit are wide awake. A wooden box was placed in the hollow of a small room in the ashram, where the man lay down in front of all the witnesses on 8 April, entered a state of *samadhi* and was then buried. The box was sealed with a lid and locked, then covered with plastic sheeting and soil, and barley seeds were planted on top to prevent any fraud. The door was locked from the outside and the ascetic was left to lie, buried in the box. On the eighth day, the door of the room in the ashram was opened, and everyone present and watching on television witnessed the beautiful green shoots growing in the soil on top of the buried yogi. The man was dug up and was fully alive. To fully come out of the state of *samadhi*, the guru began to pray and twirl the prayer beads between his fingers. He also performed a small ceremony called *puja*.

This event in the Naranarayan Baba Ashram was broadcast live on Nepali TV. The doctors who inspected the man found that all the holy man's vital signs were fine after eight days in a closed box under the soil. Dr Gautam believed such a feat was only possible by consciously shutting down the metabolism and warned ordinary people against such extreme experiments. Among yogis and ascetics, this skill is the result of long and rigorous years of meditation practice.

Guru Siddhababa is a Nepali citizen and reached enlightenment through prolonged meditation in the sacred places of Himalaya and India (information about the guru: *Himalayan Times*, 2016). There is a saying that gurus should not expose their abilities publicly, but people are so often nonbelievers. Maybe you do need a small wake-up call from time to time? After all, it's so natural to doubt in miracles, because a person often thinks that everything in this world has to be explainable, understandable and controllable.

In the morning, Maria and I took local transport again, this time a microbus taxi that happened to be missing one door, and we drove to Boudhanath again. Because it was so crowded, I sat next to the missing door, holding on tight to the edges, hoping not to slip out into the crazy traffic of Nepal's capital.

Upon arriving at the Boudhanath stupa, Maria and I did some prayer circles around the sanctuary and, soon enough, headed to the outer terrace café next to it. I took action – I had made the decision to go on pilgrimage again! I connected with Krishna, who promised to do the second pilgrimage of the season with a small discount and contacted my very good friend from whom I had to borrow some money. I was also in contact with my life partner, who thought this kind of opportunity must be seized. Everything was starting to work out.

In the evening, Krishna's brother Raj met us in the Kathmandu Guest House to settle my later plans. Departure with the Nepalese guru was supposed to take place on the 6th of August, which meant I had to spend one more week in Kathmandu on my own. I started by tackling three important things:

1. change my plane ticket booked for the next morning;
2. look for a cheaper hotel;
3. prolong my Nepalese visa.

I began to change my plane ticket for the 19th of August in the hotel garden. I tried and tried, but for some reason the Qatar airline website did not let me. Then I tried with Maria's phone, but still didn't succeed. Raj took us to the Kathmandu Guesthouse office, where they let us use their computer. I had so many thoughts in my head because of the change in my travel plans, so I asked my friend Maria to change the tickets. The computer was slow, but the thing worked – we changed the day and even entered my bank account number, but before the last click Raj's phone rang. He yelled, "Wait!" Krishna had asked us to put everything on hold for a second, because he wanted to call the Chinese officials to be sure. China quickly confirmed that I should have started my permit application to Mount Kailash three days ago. I guess somebody was watching over me, because this call came just a second before the click confirming the plane ticket. The pilgrimage to Mt Kailash with the group took place as planned. Eight months later, Baba was accused of rape (*My Republica*, March 2020). Siddhababa, on rape allegations, was given clean chit by the bench of the Justice on December 2020 (*Khabarhub*).

The ride back home

KATHMANDU (Nepal)

29/07/19, Monday – This was my last breakfast amidst the magnificent greenery of my favourite guesthouse. I ate fresh mango and sweet pastry with *chai* and let the cook make me a nice spicy omelette outside in the big hotel garden with all its scents – freshly cut grass after a night rain, ripe fruit on the trees, blooming flowers in the flowerbeds. What an amazing bouquet of aromas tickled my nostrils in the morning light.

Krishna came to the hotel, wished us *bon voyage* and ordered a taxi to the airport. The morning showed clear signs that it would be another hot July day in the capital, Kathmandu…

ॐ मणि पद्मे हूँ

Mount Kailash & Tibetan prayer flags, Tibet. Heli Grauberg, 2019

Landscape map around Mount Kailash. The lakes Manasarovar and Rakshastal and the mountain Kailash marked in red. Cartographer – Riccardo Pravettoni www.grida.no

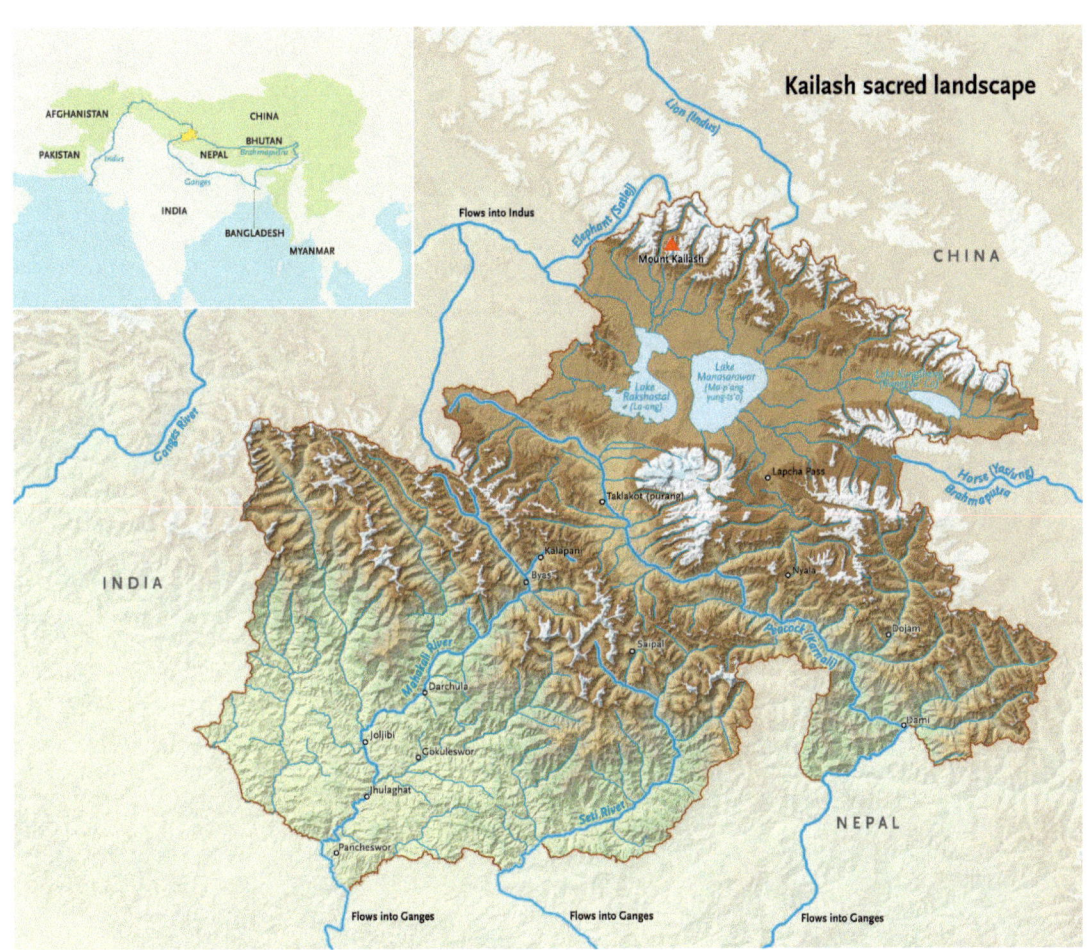

Acknowledgments

Kathmandu Holiday Tours and Travels, Krishna Dhakal, Umesh Giri, Moharaj Dhakal, Ram Gurung, Monica Sharma, Maria Palts, Meera Venkatesan, Heli Kaju, Kristiina Kütt, Dmitry Zadernovskiy, Tracey Alysson, Jyoti Subramanian, Kristina Virk, Ardashir Rahman, Erin N, Sireliis Vilu, Silvi Soo, Ain Paavo, Jussi Ollino, Helina Villem, Sirje Tambaur, Andrus Rannaääre, Man Gurung, Ujjwal Bajracharya, Ashwin Sathyamoorthy, Sultana Alam, Naima Rahman, Anwar Akbar, Angelika Sokolova, Najma Davis, Anne Sepping, Lea Nilson, Kristiina Väliste, Raivo Väliste, Swapna Sushma Patil, Evrika Ingman, Mireille Discher, Anya Rahman-Frammolino, Ralph Frammolino, Marian Geddes, Yohan Pathmanathan.

Buddha. Shutterstock, by Tjasam

"Kailash: Pilgrimages to the Tibetan Mystic Mountain"
Synopsis

This book describes a journey to holy Mount Kailash in faraway Tibet. Each year thousands of followers of Hinduism, Buddhism, Jainism and Bön make the 52-kilometer pilgrimage circuit around the 6000 meter-plus mountain. This eternally snow-covered natural pyramid is considered by some to be the center of the Universe. It is a peak that is never climbed due to its unique religious significance.

Here, Heli Grauberg describes her two 2016 & 2019 pilgrimage experiences, as well as prior events, previously visited places, and troubles that life threw her way. This is a travel book, a spiritual book, and also a practical guide for future Mount Kailash pilgrims. Between these covers you will discover why these pilgrimages are undertaken, read helpful information about Kailash travel packages, and find a list of necessities for such pilgrimages. Also included are interesting facts about Nepal and Tibet. Heli tried to put lots of photos in the book, because some marvels are not describable in words.

About the author

Heli Grauberg loves travelling, writing and photography. Her travel stories and photos have been published in Estonia's most popular weekly newspaper Eesti Ekspress and also in Estonian women and travel magazines.

Heli can often be found taking photos everywhere, and this interest came into her life during her nine years working at an international media company distributing photo rights to Estonian media.

Heli has completed yoga initiations under the guidance of Ingvar Villido (spiritual name Ishwarananda), Himalayan yogi Yogiraj Gurunath Siddhanath, and for almost 15 years yoga has been her daily wake-up routine.

The wish to see the world has been with Heli since her childhood, and her very first travels took her to Moldova, Russia and Finland. She was dreaming about a trip to Tibet, Mount Kailash for a long time, and there's a funny thing with dreams – they tend to come true.

Heli has lived in Estonia and the UK. "Kailash: Pilgrimages to the Tibetan Mystic Mountain" is her first book (first published in Estonian language 2021).

Thank you so much for purchasing this book "Kailash: Pilgrimages to the Tibetan Mystic Mountain". I hope that you enjoyed it. If so, it would be really nice if you could share this book with your friends and family by posting to Facebook & Twitter & Instagram. So that more and more people from all across the world could hear about this holy mystic Mount in the faraway land of Tibet...

I'd like to hear from you and hope that you could take some time to post a review on Amazon. Thank you,
Heli

Printed in Poland
by Amazon Fulfillment
Poland Sp. z o.o., Wrocław